QUILT
Sensations

QUILT Sensations

John Streicker & Jan Thompson

Photographs by Jonathan Gibson
and David Bircham

RAINCOAST BOOKS

Vancouver

First published in Canada in 2000 by

Raincoast Books
8680 Cambie Street
Vancouver, B.C.
V6P 6M9
(604) 323-7100

www.raincoast.com

1 2 3 4 5 6 7 8 9 10

CANADIAN CATALOGUING IN PUBLICATION DATA

Thompson, Jan, 1968-
  Quilt sensations

  Includes index.
  ISBN 1-55192-254-1

  1. Quilting. I. Streicker, John, 1962- II. Title.
TT835.T56 1999   746.46   C99-910972-3

Canadä

THE CANADA COUNCIL | LE CONSEIL DES ARTS
FOR THE ARTS | DU CANADA
SINCE 1957 | DEPUIS 1957

Raincoast Books gratefully acknowledges the support of the Government of
Canada, through the Book Publishing Industry Development Program, the
Canada Council for the Arts and the Department of Canadian Heritage. We also
acknowledge the assistance of the Province of British Columbia, through the
British Columbia Arts Council.

Designed by David Bircham
Production by Ruth Linka
Project Editor: Rachelle Kanefsky
Technical Editor: Gail Hunt

Printed and bound in Hong Kong

TABLE OF CONTENTS

INTRODUCTION

QUILTS

QUILT INSTRUCTIONS

HOW TO

LAST WORDS

INTRODUCTION

ECHOES, QUILT ECHOES
OF THE PATTERNS IN MY DREAMS
RESONATING LIFE

By taking scraps of fabric and piecing them together into simple aesthetic designs, quilts bring color,

pattern and beauty into our lives. Quilts have reached more people than any other craft in North

America. If beds are places for sleep, then quilts put the poetry of dreams into that sleep. If beds provide

us with security, then quilts add warmth to that security. They invoke feelings and memories of comfort,

home, family and tradition.

TRADITIONS

Quilting has a rich history from around the world. Most recently, the strongest developments in quilting have occurred in North America, where the tradition began as an art of necessity some 200 years ago.

Back in the 1800s, European settlers to North America found themselves in a harsh climate that demanded warm bedding. At the same time, material, typically European wools, was scarce and was needed primarily for clothing. Out of thrift, remnants of material were saved from worn-out clothing and from the cuttings of new clothes. These scraps were pieced together to make sheets of material. An insulating layer of wool batting was sandwiched between two of these sheets and then quilted to hold the batting in place.

With so many physical demands on life, it would have been easier and more efficient for North American women to produce quilts that required a minimum of effort. It's inspirational to realize that, instead, these very women took the time, care and patience to craft beautiful, durable quilts.

Aesthetic patterns were used in both piecing and quilting. The patterns were often symbolic of family, home and the natural world. Then a very simple thing happened, which changed the face of quilting: pieced patterns were uniformly sized to a repeated block. Constraining patterns so that they were based on blocks certainly did not constrain quilting. Simple variations in color, pattern or the arrangement of the blocks created a diversity of quilts. In fact, the advent of block piecing actually produced an explosion in quilting. Quilting bees formed, bringing women together. Blocks were exchanged and quilts were worked on collaboratively. In particular, quilting was often carried out by women sitting collectively around a quilt stretched across a frame. Quilts were a creative expression for women of all racial and social backgrounds.

New materials and methods were introduced into quilts. The cotton industry in the American South grew, and cotton prints and cotton batting were embraced. At the end of the 19th century, silks and velvets were used in quilting, especially in the Victorian crazy quilts. As material became more readily available, appliqué became popular. By the turn of the century, sewing machines were in many households, which made piecing easier (although most quilting was still done by hand).

Quilting declined as a craft at the close of the Great Depression. The textile industry began producing modern bed covers, and renewed prosperity meant that families could buy these bedspreads rather than make them. Furthermore, the role of women changed as they began to enter the work force during the Second World War.

Then, approximately 30 years ago, a quilting resurgence began in North America and elsewhere in the world. It's difficult to know the reasons for this revival. We think that it is because you can't supplant a creative, positive and energetic art form with mass production. Quilting is a proud tradition of women creating (and defining) art. Its appeal is that it keeps beauty and artistry close to our lives.

SENSATIONS

Today, quilting is moving in many directions at once. There are new techniques (e.g., photographic transfer), new styles (e.g., colorwash, landscape), new movements (e.g., art quilts) and broader influences from around the world (e.g., Japan, Australia). Even within "traditional" quilting, there are new materials available, an amazing number of cotton prints to choose from and endless variations on block patterns. It's an exciting time to be quilting.

The quilts featured in this book explore some interesting quilting possibilities. When we quilt, it's with a sense of wonder. We love the idea of spending time making objects that people dream under. We try to make quilts that are beautiful to look at, but we also want to create quilts that are tactile and interactive. The quilts in this book are playful, luxurious, mysterious, funky and unique. Because our quilts are not easily categorized, they're often classified as non-traditional. This is a fair assessment, but it's important to recognize that our quilts do in fact respect quilting traditions.

For example, most of our quilts are made from materials at hand: old clothes and remnants of material from friends. To us, less new material means more fabric with past associations to people and events. The use of old clothing also allows us to incorporate some fun things into our quilts, such as buttons, zippers and pockets (there's something intriguing about quilts that have little secret places!).

In motif, we usually focus on life and nature. We always personalize our quilts as much as possible, and we like to make functional, warm coverings for all. It's very rewarding to hear that our quilts, and the positive energy we put into them, help to bring about great sleeps.

A note to traditional quilters (and to other quilters, too): when you look at our quilts and find one that is inspirational, one that you would like to make, then please follow our instructions as closely or as loosely as you wish. Use our quilts to sharpen your own ideas. Change them as much or as little as you like. Use our techniques, or use those that you are more familiar or comfortable with.

A note to new quilters (and to experienced quilters, too): we believe that precision isn't the be-all and end-all of quilting. Often times, quilt instructions and instructors will stress the imperativeness of precision. More than anything, we think this emphasis on making quilts perfectly pieced or exactly square scares away prospective quilters. We would like to promote quilting rather than put it out of reach.

It's important to experiment, play and have fun with your ideas. Try it out. It doesn't make sense to worry about perfection, because there's no such thing. Although the photos make our quilts look fabulous, they do have imperfections. In fact, we've decided that the "imperfections" in our work add to the warmth and personality of the quilts. Do your best, and remember not to judge yourself too harshly.

TWO FISH

So, hello, and welcome to **Quilt Sensations**. We're Jan and John, and we're happy to present you with 15 interactive, playful, functional and downright funky quilts. Whether you're a traditional or non-traditional quilter, experienced or new to the craft, we are honored that you're here and excited to share our ideas with you.

Quilt Sensations is split into two parts: the fun part and the functional part. We begin (of course) with the fun part, in which the quilts are presented with some stunning photography. Beside each quilt photo are some stories, some poetry and various other wee tidbits of information. The stories in particular reflect some of the meaning, emotion, humor and even tragedy that went into the quilts. You'll find…

Holes to explore
Buttons galore

Weaving & waves
And rivers that rave

Fun fur & flowers
And fortunes of power

Secrets & sounds
And stars that abound

Function and fashion
With touches of passion

And fish

Jan

The latter, functional part of the book deals with how to make the quilts. In this section, comprehensive, easy-to-follow instructions and patterns are provided for each of the 15 quilts. Some of our ideas and techniques are new, and we describe them in detail. Although some of the quilts may appear quite complicated, most of the sewing is fairly simple and, in the places where techniques become tough, we suggest easier alternatives.

John

We (John and Jan) call ourselves and our quilt studio Two Fish Quilts. The name came from John's nephew Jay and his love of Dr. Seuss (you know, "One fish, two fish. Red fish, blue fish … "). In this book you'll notice the odd reference to two fish – it's our signature. In fact, we've sewn two fish into each and every quilt!

Everyone has an artistic side and everyone could use a warm covering for tranquil slumber. We hope our book will inspire you to be creative in quilting (or in other crafts) and to bring art into your life. Let your quilts express your joy, your sorrow, your world and your dreams.

Stay warm, stay well … and happy quilting.

STAY WARM,
STAY WELL

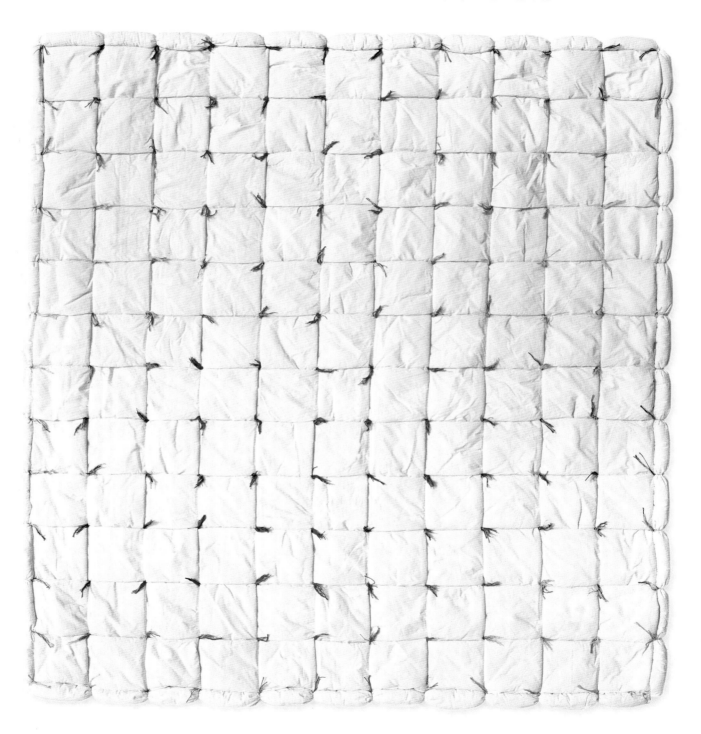

The color in this quilt is subtle. It's in the embroidery cotton, which ties the weave together.

beneath your quilt

you drift and slowly awake

and weave into your day

a little piece of your dream

you had while sleeping

beneath your quilt

you drift and slowly awake

and weave into your day

a little piece of your dream

you had while sleeping

beneath your quilt

you drift and slowly awake

and weave into your day

Stay Warm, Stay Well

September 1997

unbleached cotton, embroidery cotton

81" x 88"

From the collection of David Bircham

My grandmother was a traditional quilter…

I was sleeping under a scrap quilt of hers when I first started dreaming up quilt concepts. I was 13 years old. I kept dreaming of quilt ideas until I was 29, when I made my first quilt – a woven quilt, just like this one. You know, it was only after I made my first quilt that I discovered the definition of the term quilting.

At first glance, this quilt looks quite plain. Look again, and you will see the weaving and depth of the quilt. To us, it is really alive with movement and the natural quality of unbleached cotton. The straightforward design of this quilt allows it to be easily modified in size and color scheme. But even though it's simple, it's anything but plain. Also, it's double-thick for warmth. Stay warm, stay well.

For quilt instructions, see page 62.

LIFE IS
SWEEPING
THROUGH THE
SPACES

life is sweeping through the spaces

everything is alive

the air is alive

the silence is full of sound

the green is full of colour

light and dark chase each other

— EMILY CARR

Trees love to toss and sway...

The intrinsic beauty of nature is inspiring. Take a fir tree, for example. Not only is the whole tree stunning, but so is a single branch, so are the needles of each branch. It's amazing at all levels. Quilts mimic this natural quality by striving for beauty with each stitch, with each piece of fabric and, finally, within the entire quilt.

This quilt was inspired by the artwork and writing of Emily Carr. The title of the quilt and the quote above are taken from Emily Carr's journals, Hundreds and Thousands. The quote runs throughout the quilt, tucked away beneath enclosures of buttons (and a zipper). Explore this quilt and uncover the secret truths of nature.

For quilt instructions, see page 65.

Life Is Sweeping Through the Spaces

November 1997

assorted used materials, unbleached cotton

60" x 80"

From the collection of Mel Stidolph

Notice the ducks in the sky

The wooden buttons are meant to represent pine cones in the tree

The overall design of the quilt is our own, but it was based on the artwork of Emily Carr – a lone, beautiful tree bending to a wind swept sky

The quilt has an imaginary light source coming from the right. This effect is created in the dark-to-light sky and in the accents around the tree branches, the tree trunk and the mountains.

The cloud is made to be puffy and to sit just in front of the sky

The hills are layered to give the quilt depth

The quotes are hidden behind buttoned enclosures

This material was used once to the left of the tree and then again in reverse just below the cloud as a lighter color

These were printed denim hot pants with embroidered trim. Wow!

Jan's old, favorite shirt

KLEE WYCK

Emily Carr was an artist who painted and wrote while living among the First Nations people of the Pacific Northwest. They named her "Klee Wyck," or Laughing One.

She was born in Victoria, Canada, on December 13, 1871. Her parents died while she was in her teens. By that time, Emily Carr had shown an interest in painting. She studied in San Francisco, London and, later, in Paris, but it was with the First Nations people and in the forests that her art truly came alive. While painting, she kept journals. These journals were later published under the title Hundreds and Thousands. The quote that introduces this quilt, as well as the ones below, are taken from Emily Carr's journals.

It was these tiny things that, collectively, taught me how to live. Too insignificant to have been considered individually, but like the Hundreds and Thousands lapped up and sticking to our moist tongues, the little scraps and nothingnesses of my life have made a definite pattern. Only now, when the river has nearly reached the sea and small eddies gush up into the river's mouth and repulse the sluggish onflow, have they made a pattern in the mud flats, before gurgling out into the sea. Thank you, tiny Hundreds and Thousands. Thanks, before you merge into the great waters.

So still are the big woods, sound might not be born.

Rise into the glory of the light and air and sunshine.

Trees love to toss and sway, they make such happy noises.

*Lonesomeness
from the deeps of your soul
down among the dark silence
let your roots creep forth
gaining strength.*

Emily Carr died on March 2, 1945.

The tree trunk comes from this ribbed, stretchy zippered jumpsuit.

Seersucker Puffy Cloud

FORTUNATE

You will soon realize something.

Your life resembles a kitchen utility drawer.

Don't eat the buns.

Indecision is the key to flexibility.

You will appear in a stranger's dream tonight.

You will run amok endlessly.

Sparks will fly tonight.

Butterflies frolic in your wake…

Cheeky Monkey.

Good fortune…

One of the most enjoyable aspects of having Chinese food (apart from the wonderful food itself), is the fun of opening the fortune cookie at the end of the meal and then reading your fortune aloud to everyone assembled. We decided that it would be great if we could have fortunes at the end of every meal, no matter what kind of food we are eating. Here, fortunes are printed on unbleached cotton and attached to elastic, which is then sewn inside each placemat. A fortune can be pulled out and read at the end of every meal and then returned to its spot for your next meal. Each placemat contains 24 different fortunes, so your future holds many possibilities!

For quilt instructions, see page 70.

Fortunate

February 1999

assorted fabrics

12" x 16"

From the table of Susan Walton

& John Streicker

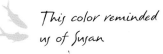

This color reminded us of Susan

Leftover fabric from Mom's turquoise dress

Leftover fabric from Jan's 'turquoise' dress

PLAYLAND

There is a place where I play,

Dreaming,

Green pastures year-round

A river running both directions at once.

My cars race the highway past fields filled with cows.

The call of the train wakes me at night –

I climb sleepily to the top of the hill,

Monsters and storms chase me back down.

I crawl into bed, the river lulling me to sleep and on

To my next adventure.

Carry a world on your shoulder...

As a child, I remember times when I would end up in those boring "adult" places and have to wait endlessly and patiently (although I'm sure I wasn't always so patient) for my parents to finish their appointments. The waiting rooms of doctors' offices and the like were generally void of any fun for children (although I did like the cartoon drawings of milk and milk products on the "Four Food Groups" poster). At present, I have noticed a definite move toward more kid-friendly offices, but it always helps to bring along some familiar playthings with you to entertain your bored tot. This quilt was designed for this very purpose. It will travel with you and your child – a ready play area always close at hand.

For quilt instructions, see page 74.

Playland

December 1998

assorted fabrics

50" x 50"

AROUND THE QUILT

The tunnel runs right through the hill

Road signs for safety on this hairpin turn

Extra batting under the fields gives a sense of dimension to the riverbank

There's also a tunnel under the river

Boats can float under the bridges

The duffel bag is attached, so the whole mat can be rolled up and taken with you

There's a pocket in the duffel bag for play cars and trains

Gold corduroy left over from an old Winnie the Pooh doll

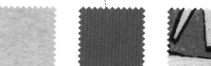

WHAT DID YOU DO TODAY?

The strangest thing happened today. This morning, when Mom was driving me to school ... no, I mean, when I was driving to my friend Joe's house, I heard a strange noise coming from my car, so I pulled off the road to investigate. As soon as I got out of the car, the wind started blowing ... I mean, it started howling. I looked down the road and saw a huge, dark cloud coming toward me very fast. It was a tornado! I looked around for shelter and saw a train tunnel. Hurry! I ran into the dark tunnel, away from the storm, and I looked out to watch it pass. But then I felt something in the darkness with me. Another person hiding from the storm? But then why wouldn't they talk to me? An animal maybe? Or a monster who can call up storms so that little kids will run into his lair? Was he waiting to eat me? But I must be too thin to satisfy a monster of that size. Well, I wasn't going to wait and find out. I turned around as quietly as I could to look into the tunnel, and I saw a small light, which was getting bigger and bigger ... Oh no! The train! Its whistle sent a shiver down my spine and, as I turned to run out, I felt something very large rush by me. I followed it outside, surprised (but a little scared, too). What could it be? But now it was dark outside, and I couldn't see what it was! Where was my car? Could I jump onto the train to escape? Then I saw a river's edge, and I ran down to it and jumped into a canoe ... no, I mean, I jumped into a motorboat and started it up. I wanted to get down the river to Joe's (what a story I had to tell Joe!), but mostly I wanted to get away from that monster. But wait! What if it isn't a monster after all, but a big, old friendly dragon that really needs someone to play with? Wouldn't Joe be surprised to see me and my new pet dragon? I circled the boat back to check, when suddenly I heard a huge splash in the river ahead of me. I couldn't see very well, but I thought I could just make out the outline of a ...

"What? Okay, Mom, I'll be down in a second ... "

Quilted green fabric adds a nice texture

Terry cloth highway

WINDSOCKS

What makes a windsock

but the cupped air,

a flag the

moving wind –

luff open your embrace

of finger-pinched ends,

upright swirls of emptiness

drops with every color

a deeper dream.

- Ryan Kuhn

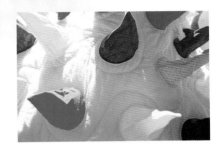

Let me make the bed...

This is a very playful quilt, both in color and in form. At each cone location, the quilt has holes cut right through all of its layers. This allows the cones to fill with air and stand at attention as the quilt is luffed…only to slow…ly… fall… back… d o w n.
You'll never have so much fun making a bed!

We made this quilt to fit the top of a double bed, but everyone always says, "This would be great for a kid's bed!" Hey, why can't adults have that fun, too?

For quilt instructions, see page 78.

Windsocks
September 1997
100% cotton, cheesecloth
56" x 75"
From the collection of David Bircham

We chose vibrant colors for a vibrant quilt

Afterwards, we noticed that we had used complimentary colors (blue and orange)

NIGHT AND DAY

I AM YOUR MOON

I am the moon.
You can't see me
because you are the sun
so full of life, so full of light,
licking the Earth, bathing the sky
with your strength and radiance
and warmth.
You project so much warmth.

I am the moon.
Beside you I wane.
In your shadow,
I am a distant echo of your voice,
a pale reflection of your brilliance.
And you can't see me.

Believe in your courage and
listen to your heart.
I am the moon.
You can't see me
but you know I am still here,
watching over you
and loving you
my daughter.

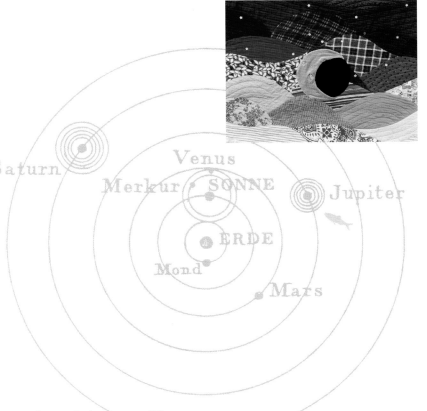

This quilt celebrates life…

The background of the quilt is a flowing patchwork that diffusely blends a dark-to-light sky at the top with rolling hills at the bottom. In the sky is the sun, brilliant giver of life, with rays that reach down to the hills and edges of the quilt. That's in the daytime, of course.

As dusk falls, you can peek behind the rays of the sun and discover tiny little stars starting to appear. At night, the sun can be completely removed from the quilt, revealing the crescent moon, receptacle of dreams.

Dream of flying, and when you awake in the morning, button the sun onto the quilt and let the rays spill back across the sky. And so the cycle of life goes…

For quilt instructions, see page 81.

Night and Day

February 1998
assorted materials with pretty star buttons
68" x 76"
From the collection of Trisha Lee Thompson

AROUND THE QUILT

Special little quilted symbols at the four corners of the quilt

The stars are mother-of-pearl buttons

These pockets still work; they're lined with extra-special flannel material

The moon has cool craters in it

The moon opens up to reveal buttons that hold the sun in place

When the sun is in place, its rays lick down to the hills and right onto the border

There are little valleys behind the hills

We all liked this purple fabric with white flowers

Of all our quilts, this one covers the color spectrum most completely

IN MEMORIAM

Quilts are an intensely personal experience. Every quilt has the ability to reflect feelings, influences and the time and effort put into making the quilt. This quilt was commissioned by Trisha Thompson, shortly after the unexpected death of her father.

When you first look at the quilt, it's all sun. The sun is bright and strong and reaches everywhere across (and even beyond) the quilt – it is very much alive, vibrant and energetic. When you remove the sun, the moon is revealed, and the quilt immediately cools down. It's not that the moon is cold or callous. On the contrary, the moon is simply quieter than the sun, more reflective. It is calming, watchful.

Now let your eyes explore right to the edges of the quilt. There you will find little pockets made of the fabric cut from pants. These pockets are lined with flannel cut from the hems of nightshirts that belonged to Trisha's father, mother and grandmother. The pockets are therefore very personal little hiding spots. They are tiny, safe havens for secrets to be cherished and held close.

Now go back to the sun and the moon in both the quilt and the accompanying poem. The sun symbolizes Trisha and the moon symbolizes her father, Edward George Thompson, born November 19, 1940, died September 11, 1996.

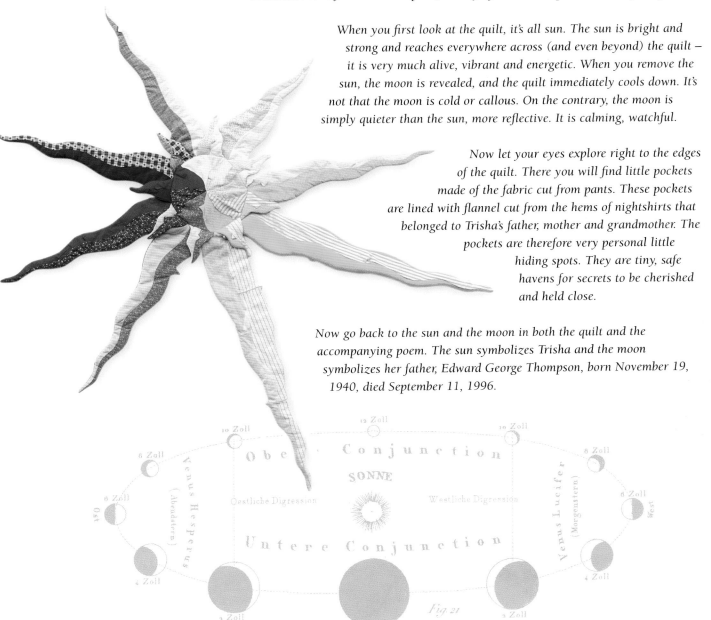

Every time you cut this velvet, you end up with a silvery glitter on other fabrics nearby

Poor orange... on this quilt it's the least represented color from the spectrum

25

WEE BAIRN

Polar Fleece™ for a soft sleep.

McLeod tartan.

Denim represents a Saskatchewan farming background.

A new day begins with your smile imprinted on my mind
Your laugh I carry through the hardships of my day
My strength improves as I hold you in my arms
*   showing you this new world.*

There has been a change in everyone around you
There is a new glow, a new softness in our looks
*   as we gaze at you*
We collect and thrive on the energy you grant us.
This gift you give unknowingly
This new joy in our lives.

The rolling clouds unfold the awaiting patient moon
*   as a new day ends.*
I tuck you in and brush my fingers against your warm cheeks
Your feet and hands so tiny, your movements so strong
The moon shines on my starry eyes.

The gift of life for you, and a rebirth for me.
*   I will always grow with you.*

A quilt to capture memories…

This baby quilt was specially made for friends of ours and their newborn child, Ella. We wanted to make a non-traditional baby quilt that was bright and colorful and that had some interesting tactile fabrics and fun things to play with. Ella's parents, who had some great ideas that they wished to incorporate into the quilt, helped us out with the design.

Wee Bairn

April 1999

assorted fabrics, Polar Fleece™, berber

40" x 40"

From the crib of Ella Chicilo McLeod

The quilt is made in the shape of a large flower, with nine petals surrounding the center. Each petal reveals something about the family, such as their names, the symbols associated with Ella's time of birth (lion's paw = Leo, tiger's paw = Year of the Tiger) and the landscapes that are meaningful to them (prairies, mountains and ocean). The whole quilt is drawn together by the three hearts that link the three members of the family. The end result is a very personal, fun and functional quilt for Ella.

For quilt instructions, see page 86.

CABIN FEVER

Rainy Sunday afternoon

Don't want to go outside

Can't imagine getting anything done

Perfect time for a game!

For 2 or more players

Ages 6 and up

Pick your team

Set up the game pieces

Shuffle the cards

Choose your marker

Roll a die to see who starts.

Aces high, roll again, do not pass go.

Lose your turn, send the other player back, checkmate!

Highest score, most pieces, first across the line wins.

In case of a draw, begin it all again!

It's all fun and games...

Life often seems to be one big competition. We compete in school, at work, when driving home, in reaching for that last box of frosty-crunchy-oaty cereal. The competitive spirit does seem to be alive and well in the world. So why not bring a little of it (in a good-natured, fun sense, of course) into the bedroom? This reversible quilt includes the old standards – chess, checkers, backgammon, cribbage – to challenge you and your mate. All the game pieces, dice, cards, etc. are stored in pockets that hang down over the edges of the bed. Or, take this playful quilt out of the bedroom and enjoy a quick game after your picnic lunch.

Now, what will be the forfeit for the loser?

For quilt instructions, see page 89.

Cabin Fever

December 1998
assorted fabrics
54" x 72"
(80" x 72" with pockets)

AROUND THE QUILT

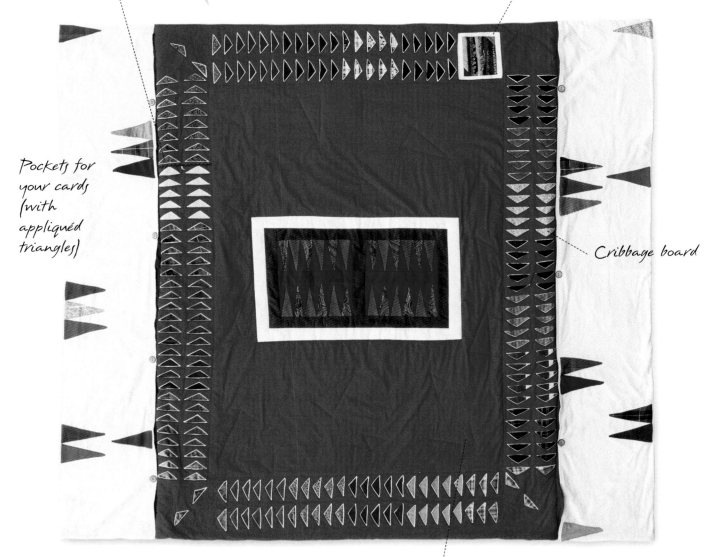

Skunk line
(how humiliating!)

Backgammon board
in the center

Finishing square for the
cribbage winner

Pockets for
your cards
(with
appliquéd
triangles)

Cribbage board

Triangles quilted at
random locations

Jan's (and her sister's)
old, favorite dress

Wine-colored corduroy for the
backgammon board

Scraps from a dress that
never got hemmed

Game marker squares with instructions tucked inside

Chess/checkerboard in the center

Start and finish the board game at the star

Easy-to-cut Saskatchewan shapes!

Generic board game

Pockets for checker and chess pieces

Squares quilted at random locations

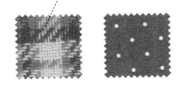

An old, warm wool scarf

Green velvet for the chessboard

Leftovers from a 1970s polyester project

TANGIBLE

In order to assist you in imagining how nice these squares are to touch, we have added some sound effects

Ooohhh

Mmmmmm

drift through nothingness

traverse an emptiness

reach for contact

until

tangential impact

a tendril of feeling

and senses are reeling

sensuous undulations, velvety passion

satin caresses, tender compassion

emotions surface a love untold

sentiments linger continue to hold

touch

and a gentler touch as sensations unfold

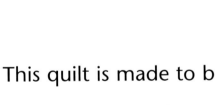

This quilt is made to be touched…

It is pure tactiledom! It has little wavy outdents and little "pokey" indents. Then there are the big squares of solid fabric to luxuriate in.

Originally the quilt was inspired by the game of Twister™, so we adapted a set of rules that would allow two people to play on this tangible quilt. One person is designated to call out types of fabric. The other person is designated to call out body parts. On the count of three, each calls out a choice. Then both players have to move the chosen body part onto the chosen square of fabric. Last one "uncollapsed" wins.

More risqué quilters (than us) might even suggest that adults could play this game blindfolded and naked!

For quilt instructions, see page 94.

Tangible

February 1999
velvet, corduroy, peach skin, berber,
faux fur, brushed cotton.
63" x 78"
From the collection of Jacqueline Robins
(potter extraordinaire).

Aaahhh

BABY BEAR HUG

I wonder

do you dream of bears
sleeping in the wood
would you dream of bear hugs
I really think you should

do you dream of fireflies
winking in the night
do you soar with swallows
ribbons in the light

do you float with guppies
and dream without a sound
or do you nap with puppies
all flopped upon the ground

do you dream of me
I wonder if you do
I am your mother
all my dreams are you

Every newborn deserves a special quilt…

Years ago, when my first niece was just starting to talk, she walked up and gave me a big hug on my leg. I hugged her back too hard, and in a concerned voice she said, "Squeeze!" Ever since, I've looked for ways to express my love to young people without overpowering them. This quilt is a metaphor for a big, protective, loving hug. Can't you just picture a baby wrapped up in it?

Of all our quilts, this one is closest to a traditional patchwork. Still, it's not quite traditional. The bearpaws and feet are made like little mittens, which can serve as fun puppets in a pinch. It can also be used as a costume, or as a tantalizing little sleeping mat that would look beautiful anywhere. But which side to sleep on? Fun fur versus flannel, bum up versus bum down? Every baby (and adult) will have a preference.

For quilt instructions, see page 98.

Baby Bear Hug

September 1998
assorted flannels, faux fur
approx. 28" x 42"

AROUND THE QUILT

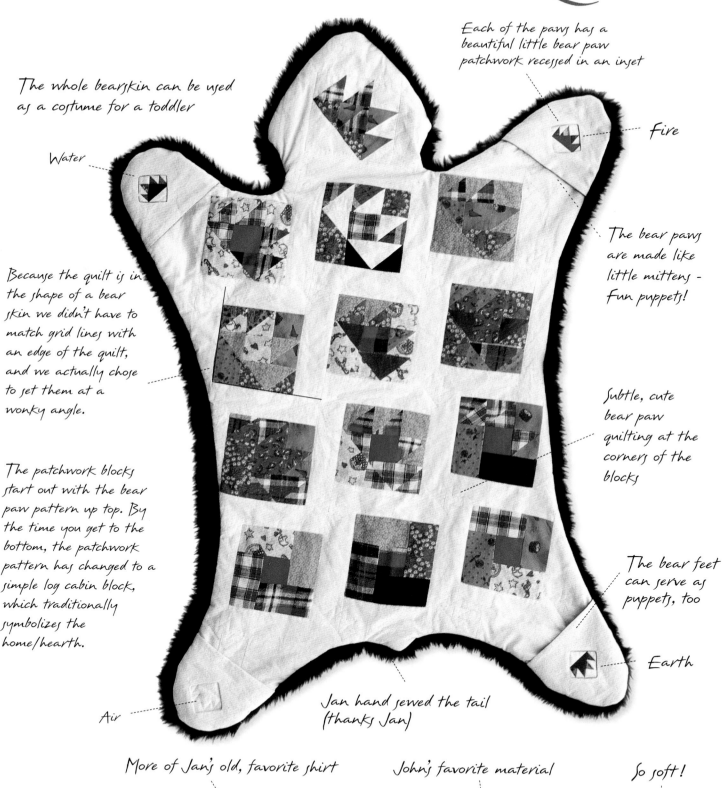

The whole bearskin can be used as a costume for a toddler

Each of the paws has a beautiful little bear paw patchwork recessed in an inset

Water

Fire

Because the quilt is in the shape of a bear skin we didn't have to match grid lines with an edge of the quilt, and we actually chose to set them at a wonky angle.

The bear paws are made like little mittens - Fun puppets!

Subtle, cute bear paw quilting at the corners of the blocks

The patchwork blocks start out with the bear paw pattern up top. By the time you get to the bottom, the patchwork pattern has changed to a simple log cabin block, which traditionally symbolizes the home/hearth.

The bear feet can serve as puppets, too

Earth

Air

Jan hand sewed the tail (thanks Jan)

More of Jan's old, favorite shirt

John's favorite material

So soft!

THE FOUR ELEMENTS

Baby Bear Hug *was designed, and the accompanying lullaby was written, using the four elements as inspiration. The quilt is meant to reflect the inherent qualities of the four elements and to instill these very qualities in a newborn child.*

FIRE

- 🐾 *Heart, Hearth, Warmth*
- 🐾 *The centers of the patchwork blocks are in red tones, representing Fire and respecting the log cabin block tradition*
- 🐾 *Mother's Love, Lifeblood of the Baby*
- 🐾 *Passion*

WATER

- 🐾 *The Womb, Birth*
- 🐾 *The second ring of the patchwork blocks are in blues, representing Water*
- 🐾 *Pregnancy, Mother and Baby as One*
- 🐾 *Wisdom*

EARTH

- 🐾 *Home, Foundation, Body*
- 🐾 *The entire backing of the quilt is in a rich brown, representing Earth*
- 🐾 *Mother Earth, Mother Bear, Baby Bear*
- 🐾 *Strength, Life*

AIR

- 🐾 *Sleep, Dreams, Soul*
- 🐾 *The sashing in between the blocks, laid out in a windmill pattern, represents Air*
- 🐾 *Mother's Breath, Baby's Breath*
- 🐾 *Creativity, Spirituality*

John's Christmas gift, 1993
(I meant to tell you, Mum and Dad, that I really liked this shirt, but it shrunk a little too much for me)

Jan's favorite material

We chose a super-rich fun fur. 'Fun fur' sounds way too plain. 'Funnest fur? 'Fabulous fur?

FISH on FRIDAYS

海は広いな大きいな
月が昇るし日が沈む

The sun sinks slowly
into the peaceful ocean,
the moon a shy smile

We seem to have a preoccupation with fish...

We both grew up on the Canadian Prairies. As children, a fish dinner for us was fish sticks. We've broadened our fish horizons since then, but I'm not sure it explains our fascination with… but we digress.

Gyotaku, the ancient Japanese practice of fish printing, is an art form that developed as a means of recording species of fish, something like John Audubon and his paintings of birds. Normally the fish printing is done onto paper, but the technique works very well on fabric. These funky quilted fish prints double as pot holders and trivets.

For quilt instructions, see page 102.

Fish on Fridays

January 1999

cotton, acrylic paint

8½" x 8½"

CLASSIC THEATER

PROLOGUE

Fish Sorting Factory

PENGUIN: [Singing] *You're my sweet little buttercup…*

OCTOPUS: *Son, son. What are you doing? Look at this mess. All of the guppies are mixed in with the halibut. Oh, what senseless tragedy! Why, oh why, do you insist on daydreaming and singing sentimental ditties? Look at giraffe there, she works hard.*

PENGUIN: *I try to concentrate father, but my heart yearns for the outdoors. Oh, to be in a field with wild flowers and lovely insects, where the hills are alive.* [Begins to sing…]

OCTOPUS: *Son, son. This isn't some alpine meadow. This is a fish sorting factory. This is our fish sorting factory, your future. Commerce, economics and fish, son. Why, for generations, we octopi have run a reputable and profitable fish sorting business, and when I retire you will be the king fish.*

PENGUIN: *Me? Why not giraffe?*

OCTOPUS: *Giraffe? Sure, giraffe works hard, but she doesn't have the dexterity to sort the smaller fish. Besides, she's not my adopted son … Oops.*

PENGUIN: *Adopted! So the truth is out. You are not my father, and this is not my destiny.* [Exit Penguin]

The crowd hushes in anticipation…

The house lights are dimmed. The curtain rises. Enter stage left Ladybug and Penguin side by side, and instantly we are swept up into the saga of their struggle with Mad Cow and the turbulent love affair that ensues. High operatic drama to be sure.

This quilt is a rich draping of purple velvet with "floopy dagging" (see "Around the Quilt," page 42) and gold embroidered scrolls, complete with a stage, curtain and dressing rooms for our thespian … finger puppets. This quilt works equally well as a permanently hung finger puppet theater or on a bed with the theater in the center (i.e., be both the stage manager and the audience at once). Jan fell in love with this puppet theater quilt, so it has become part of her collection.

For quilt instructions, see page 105.

Classic Theater

January 1999
velvet
56" X 63"
From the collection of Jan Thompson

The top is made to slide onto a curtain rod for easy hanging

Curtains open and close and snap shut

Zippers in the pennants act as dressing rooms for our thespian finger puppets

Different backdrops can be snapped into place

Banners can be moved around and placed on the front or back

At the fabric shop, we were discussing the pennants with the store clerk, and she said that a row of pennants is called dagging. We went on to discuss the stiffness of the dagging, and she suggested that we use a firm lining, or else we would have "floopy dagging." We thought this was an excellent phrase, and we told her we were going to try to include it in our book. "Floopy dagging."

ACT I

Alpine Meadow

PENGUIN: *Winds through the olive trees softly did blow …* [Enter Ladybug, landing near Penguin] *Hello.*

LADYBUG: *Hello. That was a lovely song.*

PENGUIN: *Thank you. I love to sing.*

LADYBUG: *Tell me, do you like insects?*

PENGUIN: *Oh yes, I love dragonflies and bumble bees and fireflies and ladybugs and …*

LADYBUG: *I'm a ladybug.*

PENGUIN: [Startled] *Really?*

LADYBUG: [Coyly] *Really.*

PENGUIN: *I love you.* [Enter Mad Cow and Duck]

MAD COW: *Wait, wait, you can't be in love with each other yet. I've just arrived to woo you Ladybug.*

PENGUIN: *Woo who?*

LADYBUG: *Don't cry darling, I love you and no other.*

MAD COW: *But Ladybug, you promised to accompany me to the lower pasture. At least grant me this.*

LADYBUG: *Oh, all right.*

PENGUIN: *I will wander off with Duck and return anon.* [Penguin kisses Ladybug]

DUCK: *What is a "Non"?* [Exit Penguin and Duck]

MAD COW: [Aside] *Now Ladybug is mine. I have tricked Duck into leading Penguin to his death, and then it will be me that she weds.*

LADYBUG: *Let us hurry then Cow. I can't wait to see my Penguin again.*

MAD COW: [Aside] *It will be sooner than she thinks.* [Exit Ladybug and Mad Cow]

ACT II

Cliff Above Lower Pasture

PENGUIN: *I'm on the top of the world, looking down on …* [Stops singing] *Whoa, we're high up, aren't we?*

DUCK: *Not really. After all, you can fly.*

PENGUIN: *Fly? Why, no. I don't think so.*

DUCK: *Sure you can. You are a member of the bird family, aren't you?*

PENGUIN: *Well, I'm not exactly sure what I am. Up until today, I thought I was an octopus.*

DUCK: *Well, you've got wings, so all you need to do is flap them, like this.* [Duck flaps]

PENGUIN: [Tries jumping up and fails] *I guess it's not for me.*

DUCK: *Oh, that's too bad, because the cow told me that Ladybug could only love someone who flies.*

PENGUIN: *Then I must fly!*

DUCK: *You probably just need more air time to get it right.*

PENGUIN: *All right then here I go.* [Jumps off cliff] *Laaaadyyyybuuu …* [Exit Penguin]

DUCK: *Oh, what have I done?*

ACT III

Lower Pasture

PENGUIN: *aaaadyyyybuuug …* [Enter Penguin]

LADYBUG: *Oh my darling, you are falling to a gruesome death at my six feet.*

MAD COW: *Ha ha, ha ha, moooo!*

GHOST: [Enter Ghost saving Penguin] *I am the good ghost of adopted penguins, and I have come to save you.*

PENGUIN: *You mean, I'm a Penguin?*

LADYBUG: *Oh Penguin, how did this happen?*

DUCK: [Enter Duck] *I'm so sorry. Cow told me to help you learn how to fly.*

LADYBUG: *A disease on you Cow and all your milk. Come Penguin, let us be wed and sing.* [Exit Ladybug and Penguin]

GHOST: *Come Cow, and don't be mad. Let me attend your sickness.* [Exit Cow and Ghost]

DUCK: [Soliloquy] *Alas, will I never be able to exploit my unbridled talent as a small fish sorter? And will I never find the giraffe of my dreams?* [Curtain]

TSUNAMI

ocean sleeps light

There's a small cliff down by the bay —
a sandstone battlement
crumbling in testimony to the ocean's might.

The weathered rock burns ochre
against the sunset deep sea
brooding cold calm, for now —
waiting for the moon's next courting.

But the ocean sleeps light
and come dawn
when the young breeze pushes landward
this seascape wakes from a lazy salt drift
to the beat of whitecaps crashing;
a pounding relentless
along this broken shore.

This whole coastline tells
of quiet battles fought and lost,
of land retreating
from the ocean
at a rate measured in lifetimes.

— JONATHAN GIBSON

Quilts have rhythms…

The aesthetic of quilts comes from taking scraps of material and translating them into functional works of art. Beds – warm dream havens – deserve nothing less than a quilt of your making. But, where else do we indulge in soothing relaxation? The answer, of course, is the tub.

A lot of thinking is done in the shower: dreaming up schemes, planning days, contemplating life. That's why this design is so exciting: a quilted shower curtain of radiant sea glass. Your water bills will be going up!

For quilt instructions, see page 110.

Sea glass, or "beach" glass, is human garbage that the oceans have made beautiful.

Tsunami

December 1998
glass, shell, stone, plastic, netting
28" x 33"
From the collection of Erin Dolman
& Eric Allen Montgomery

45

BUDDING POET

A quilt that grows…

We originally called this quilt "Budding Artist" because we envisioned a number of pieced blocks that could be arranged and rearranged into larger works of art. As it turned out, we decided to use words instead, so the blocks now function more like fridge-magnet poetry. You can choose words to suit your moods and then button them together to create poetry, phrases, advice or just utter nonsense. The resulting piece may be a rectangular quilt or a free-form poetry hanging for the wall. On the back of each square is a Drunkard's Path block, perhaps subconsciously chosen to complement the angst-ridden poet in all of us!

For quilt instructions, see page 112.

Budding Poet
February 1999
cotton, assorted fabrics, "orphan" buttons
42" x 56"

AROUND THE QUILT

Drunkards Path block

Words can be printed onto fabric in a number of ways

Rearrange the words as you wish

make your sigh believe

ripe with two fish curls

go to around

my aqua

The blocks are held together at the corners using "orphan" buttons — buttons that have lost their brothers and sisters...

Every block is reversible

John's favorite material

Arrange the blocks into any shape

awaken after beautiful sleep

We made this arrangement reversible

arouse my tender spirit with your embrace

dream infinite the believe make and

to

Our green-and-purple color scheme was inspired by a quilt found
in a book that showcased Japanese quilters

Hand-dyed piece donated by Joy —
a glass artist with a textile art past

We have tons of old
plaid flannel shirts

An ex-pullover —
nice and fuzzy

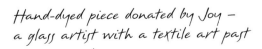
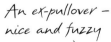

BUNNIES IN THE GARDEN

See the little bunny,

the bunny's in the carrot,

the carrot's in the garden,

the garden's in the hills.

See the purple turnip,

right beside the carrot,

in between the onion

and radish that is red.

See the little bunnies

hide behind the flowers,

the flowers in the garden,

the garden in the fields.

See the pretty hilltops,

underneath the white clouds,

floating in the blue sky,

it's all atop my bed.

Bunnies in the Garden

October 1998

assorted fabrics, "orphan" buttons

60" x 80"

From the bed of wee Colette McIsaac

Cute, cuddly and educational…

This quilt has little bunnies living in and around a vegetable garden. More than just fun, this quilt is also designed to help little minds learn. It's packed full of educational opportunities, such as teaching wee ones how to use buttons and zippers, how to differentiate between near and far and much more. Most of all, though, this quilt can be used to help children learn how to count.

There's one moon. There are five clouds in the sky and six rays on the sun. The flowers are grouped in threes, and each one has two sides (and five petals). The vegetable garden has four rows. Each row has 10 pockets and 10 vegetables, including one humongous carrot with one big zipper. Eleven bunnies live inside the carrot. So in total, there's one moon, one sun, five clouds, 10 spring onions, 10 radishes, 10 carrots, 10 turnips, 11 bunnies, 40 flowers, plus two fish for good measure. And that makes 100!

For quilt instructions, see page 115.

AROUND THE QUILT

Sun and moon rise and set behind the hills

Secret bunny hiding spots (ssshhhh – don't tell!)

Flowers are sewn on but they're made to flip so that you can change the color scheme of the floral arrangement

Clouds are buttoned on so that they can spin, flip or drift around to other buttons

Vegetables go from medium-small to ultra-teeny cute

The centers of the flowers are another good home for "orphan" buttons

Backing was hand-dyed and had a simple counting poem embroidered into it

Old long johns – now that's recycling!

A COUNTING QUILT

1 quilt with 2 sides,

4 corners and blue skies.

In the sky, a moon and sun

and clouds to hide either one.

The sun and rain make things grow

on the hills down below.

3 fields on every hill,

far away and closer still.

40 flowers with 40 middles,

200 petals, big to little.

In between a garden lies,

everything a different size.

4 rows of hidden wonder.

Pull the stalks to see what's under.

10 spring onions, green and white,

stand straight up on the right.

10 radishes, red and round,

on the left, in the ground.

10 turnips out they pop,

with bumps and eyes and purple tops.

9 carrots in a row,

plus 1 more big one down below.

In this carrot is something funny.

Zip it open – there's a bunny.

Just a minute, there's another,

a furry little bunny brother.

And another, there's even more,

1, 2, 3 … 4!

Bunny sisters, bunny brothers

and, oh my goodness, there's still others.

5, 6, 7, 8,

9, 10, 11… Wait!

I'd like to play. I'd like to hop

but I'm so tired, I have to stop.

It's time to put my friends away.

I'll count again another day.

I'd like to rest, I'd like to sleep,

I'd like to dream of counting sheep.

Goodnight sun, goodnight moon.

Goodnight Mom, I'll see you soon.

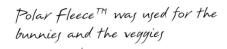

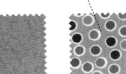

Polar Fleece™ was used for the bunnies and the veggies

Flowers were made using scraps from many different fabrics (around 50)

Corduroy works so well when you want to have projecting lines in a landscape

HOW TO

This section is devoted to showing you how to create the quilts that we presented in the first part of the book. Remember that when we provide instructions, they're not necessarily meant to be used as strict guidelines, but rather as examples of how you might accomplish the sewing. At all stages of each quilt, you will need to make some of the design decisions, from choosing fabric to deciding the length of your quilting stitch. We always encourage you to take as much initiative as you wish. Whether you follow our designs closely, use only some of our ideas or use our quilts as inspiration for your own designs, we hope that our quilts and these instructions will prompt you to be creative in your quilting, and even in your life in general.

These first few "How To" pages are devoted to describing some basic aspects of sewing, which are general to quilting. We finish this section with a description of some sewing techniques, which are particular to our quilts.

A note on terminology to first-time quilters: Sometimes the term quilting is used to refer to the entire process of making a quilt and sometimes it is used to refer to the process of stitching through all of the layers of a quilt. The context in which the term is used will enable you to differentiate between the two.

Equipment

One of the things that has made quilts so accessible over the years is that they are possible to create using minimal equipment: a pair of scissors and a needle. Today, however, quilts are being made more and more by machine. In fact, the quilts in this book were made mostly by machine. If we fail to state otherwise in a set of instructions, you can assume that the quilt was machine-pieced and machine-quilted. Nevertheless, it is quite possible to make many of our quilts by hand, and we encourage you to decide which method is best for you and your quilt.

Machines

We used two sewing machines to make the quilts – one standard Kenmore™ that Jan's Grannie bought for her when she was 19, and one industrial Pfaff™ that we call Edith. This second machine gives us the advantage of being able to sew through many layers of fabric fairly easily. A slightly longer arm also means that it is easier to finish the top quilting by machine. However, with a little clever maneuvering and fewer shortcuts, all the quilts featured in this book can be done on a conventional home sewing machine.

Other Equipment

Other equipment that is typically used:
- A good pair of cloth scissors.
- An iron and ironing board.
- A rotary cutter and mat (time-saving but not absolutely necessary).
- Rulers, soft-leaded pencils, chalk.
- Pins, needles, safety pins.
- A walking foot (a special sewing machine foot that helps to feed layers of fabric more evenly).
- A seam ripper (not that you'll ever use it!).
- Books and magazines for ideas and inspiration (and not just on quilting!).
- Cookies.

Some non-traditional equipment that we have found useful:
- Tweezers, chopsticks, crochet hooks (for turning).
- Masking tape, hockey tape (as a stitching template that adheres to fabric without pinning).
- Music.

Materials

The basic materials in a quilt are fabric and batting, which are held together with thread. From time to time, quilts might also use bias tape, embroidery cotton and/or yarn. We use all these materials and more. We also use zippers, buttons, snaps, elastic, lace, jingle bells, sea shells, sea glass...

Fabric

Quilters today can choose from a spectrum of colors and patterns in easy-to-sew, 100% cotton fabrics. Although we too use these beautiful cottons in our projects, we often try to explore the amazing variety of materials beyond lightweight cottons. Our quilts contain scraps of corduroy, Polar Fleece™, fun fur, knitted materials, stretch velvet, denim… Basically, if a fabric can survive a machine wash and dry, we'll use it.

We use a lot of second-hand clothing. It's a more economical and environmental approach to quilting – reduce, reuse, recycle. Most of the fabric that we use has either been donated by friends or bought as used clothing from a local thrift store (in 10-lb bags). Scraps of old, favorite clothing are added to our quilts for that extra bit of familiarity. These pieces give us a continuity with and respect for our past. It reminds us of our grandmothers' quilts, which had familiar scraps of fabric left over from all of their sewing projects. Quilts are the perfect place for making use of these leftover pieces, or for making one final "show" of that favorite shirt that is now horribly out of fashion (oh, that fickle mistress – fashion).

When we use old clothing in our quilts, we like to include the buttons, zippers and pockets, too. They make great little hiding places for treasures and secrets. However, they're not always easy to work with. Also, stretchy, slippery or heavy fabrics may be more difficult to sew, and the final result may look a little lumpier than a traditional quilt. However, we think this makes the quilting process more fun and interesting. Often, we purposely design our quilts **not** to be flat. In fact, we often focus on making our quilts a tactile experience.

Of the fabrics that we do buy, the one we use the most is 100% unbleached cotton. You'll see this material in our backings and borders. Unbleached cotton has a very natural look and feel, and we love the way it wears after the first few washings.

Color

When it comes to colors, choose ones that you like. We use a lot of shades in the green-blue spectrum. If you're not sure what to choose, you can often find colors that you like by looking at fabrics or other quilts that appeal to you, or by flipping through books (we keep our favorite art books right in our quilting studio). Another good source for color is the world around you, and especially nature.

Once in a while, we force ourselves to branch out into other color schemes. It's great to explore and, in the end, these fresh color schemes have worked really well for us. We love bright, bold colors and fabulous textures in our fabric. We have an idea that someday we'll make an "over the top" quilt that will use every color (and then some) in all sorts of bizarre combinations (for this quilt, we'll definitely have to use a fringe of dingle balls around the border).

Batting

In most of our quilts we use a 7-oz polyester batting. In some cases, we use two layers of batting for an extra-thick, warm quilt. At some points, we have also split the batting in half for a lighter finished product. The choice is yours – a lighter weight may not be as warm, but it will be easier to work with due to less bulk. Cotton batting may also be used for a flatter quilt (it has a lower loft or puffiness), but it must be quilted at a closer interval, and it tends to be more expensive and doesn't stand up as well to repeated washings. As alternatives to batting, we used Polar Fleece™ in our placemats and heat shield in our pot holders.

The Size of Your Quilt

After you have chosen a quilt project, the first thing you need to do is decide what size you wish to make your quilt. You can make your quilt the same size as we made ours, or you can adjust the size. Most quilts are based on patterns, and they can be adjusted in size by scaling the pattern up or down, or by increasing or reducing the number of repetitions in the pattern. Note: Throughout the book, we use measurements in inches. For metric conversions, refer to the chart below.

Generally, quilts are made to sit on top of the bed or with the borders of the quilt draping over the sides. Standard mattress sizes are listed in the table below.

Standard Mattress Sizes

Crib	27" x 52"
Twin	39" x 75"
Double	54" x 75"
Queen	60" x 80"
King	76" x 80"

If the size of the quilt that you wish to make is different than the size that we have made ours, then you need to do one of three things. First, you can scale the whole quilt to a larger or smaller size. It's possible to do this with any of our quilts. Second, for those quilts with a repeated pattern (e.g., **Stay Warm, Stay Well; Baby Bear Hug; Windsocks; Tangible; Tsunami;** and **Budding Poet**), you can add or reduce the number of rows in the pattern. Third, for those quilts that are pieced until they reach a final size (e.g., **Life Is Sweeping Through the Spaces; Night and Day; Playland;** and **Bunnies in the Garden**), you can just decide what you want the final size to be.

Warning: If you plan to scale one of our quilts down for use as a baby quilt, then it's imperative that you make a quilt that does **not** have removable objects, large stitches or loose areas that a baby can get caught up in.

Scaling and Templates

Where templates are possible, we have supplied them. **Unless otherwise indicated, use templates to full scale.** When we are working with templates, we often transfer them to a piece of paper and then cut them out. In order to transfer them, we either trace or draft them. If you decide to photocopy our templates, make sure that there is no distortion in the copy.

There are some great alternatives to paper templates that we like to use. For drawing or cutting templates, we like to use thin cardboard, such as the cardboard that cereal boxes are made of. For quilting or stitching templates, we sometimes use tape. We draw the pattern onto the tape and then cut it out. Then we stick the tape onto the fabric (without pinning) and stitch around it. The tape might last five to 10 times before it will not adhere to the fabric anymore. Contact paper or shelf liner also works as an alternative to tape.

Where templates are far too large for the size of the pages of this book, we have not included them. In these instances, you can create templates by using the diagrams provided in one of a number of ways. First, you can use an opaque projector to project and then trace the diagram onto a large piece of paper or a sheet of fabric. If you don't have access to an opaque projector, then you can copy the diagram onto acetate and use an overhead projector. Second, you can enlarge the graph in the diagram by drawing a bigger version of it onto a large piece of paper or a sheet of fabric. Then, using this graph as a guide, you can draw the quilt layout by hand, one square at a time. Of course, if you wish, we encourage you to use our diagram only as a guide and to freehand sketch your own layout. Finally, if the real size of the template is not too much larger than the diagram, then you might be able to simply use a photocopier to enlarge the diagram.

Remember, though, that when you are scaling, you will still want to maintain a $1/4$" seam allowance in most cases.

METRIC CONVERSION TABLE

1 meter = 39.37 inches
1 yard = 36 inches
1 inch = 2.54 centimeters

yards x 0.9144 = meters
inches x 2.54 = centimeters

Basic Steps in Quilt-Making

In these next few paragraphs we review the basic steps involved in making our quilts, highlighting our particular style and choices.

Before You Begin – Prewashing Fabric

Make sure that all of your fabric is prewashed before you begin. This will take care of shrinkage and **should** take care of excess dye that isn't held in the fabric. We wash all our fabric in cold-water cycles with a small piece of unbleached cotton, so it will be evident if any dye is coming out of the fabric pieces. Dry everything on a medium setting in the dryer.

Fabric bought in stores is generally colorfast, as are secondhand clothes that have been well loved and well washed. However, some fabrics, especially dark reds, blues, greens and purples, are particularly susceptible to bleeding. Never take any chances – a fabric that bleeds is much easier to take care of **before** the quilt is assembled (see "Quilt Woes," page 122).

If we have a fabric that bleeds, we do one of three things. We (1) wash it repeatedly until it no longer bleeds; (2) wash it in a chemical such as Synthrapol™, which will bond with the free dye particles; or (3) we don't use the fabric at all.

Cutting and Piecing

Normally quilters cut material to exact shapes based on the pattern they are using plus a $1/4"$ seam allowance. These precut pieces can be pieced together using the edge of the material as a guide in stitching the seam. Quite often we do things the other way around, piecing first with an oversized piece of fabric (but not so large that it is unmanageable), and cutting the seam allowance after.

Here are examples of when we choose to cut **after** we piece:

- We often use odd-shaped or irregular-sized piecing, so it's easier to mark a line with a pencil, stitch the seam and then cut the seam allowance to make a clean finish.
- Because we use scraps of clothing, we don't always get the grain going in the best direction. In instances where the grain is not in line with the seam, it's easier to work a little further in from a rough edge than $1/4"$.
- We often stitch many layers of fabric together, and it's difficult to get all the seams to line up. It's easier to piece all of the layers together and then trim them evenly afterwards.
- We also use heavier fabrics, and some of them are really tricky to sew $1/4"$ from the unfinished edge. If you piece first, you can sew further in from the unfinished edge and trim the seam allowance afterwards.
- Sometimes we want to see how a material behaves as we're sewing it. In these instances, we don't precut the pieces exactly, so if a problem arises, there's a chance to compensate and adjust the direction of the seam.

In the instructions, we give you the dimensions of the pieces and/or templates for cutting the material precisely. Where we've employed our "piece first, cut second" strategy, we let you know. It's completely up to you to decide how you want to proceed. Both methods can, and will, work – we've simply chosen what works best for us.

Unless otherwise stated, all seam allowances are $1/4"$.

Quilting and Finishing

For 7-oz polyester batting, the recommended interval between quilting lines is 8" or less. In some of our projects, our quilt lines are further apart than this recommendation (sometimes we quilt to intervals of 10", rebels that we are). We haven't run into any trouble with batting bunching up around the quilting lines, and we trust the space-age technology of our polyester batt to continue to hold up. However, if you are not so sure and are more of a low-risk investor, you might want to quilt at a more acceptable interval. Read the recommendations on the bags of batting that you buy.

Another thing that we often do is quilt through the top sheet and the batting only (quilting before the backing goes onto the quilt). We were uncertain of this at first, worried that the sewing machine wouldn't be able to handle it, or that the batting would get caught in the feed dogs. However, nothing ventured, nothing gained: we tried it, and it works very well indeed. For example, in **Life Is Sweeping Through the Spaces** (page 65), we used this technique to do the first quilting, then we added another layer of batting and the backing and did a few more quilting lines through the whole quilt. This way, the quilting gave the quilt two levels of texture.

Our choice of quilting is often very simple, following the lines of the piecing or emphasizing the pattern of the pieced front. We like to give our quilts depth and contrast, hence we usually choose a less dense quilting interval and more batting.

Polar Fleece™ is an exciting new option as a batting material. It's a great insulator and can be environmentally friendly, as some of the newer Polar Fleece™ is made from recycled plastics. With Polar Fleece™, you can choose to not quilt at all (because it won't pull apart like batting), or you can choose to quilt a lot (because it is very easy to work with). Polar Fleece™ can be used as both the batting and backing of the quilt, thus saving on material. It makes a beautifully soft underbelly for a quilt.

Traditionally, quilts are finished by putting the whole quilt together and then binding the edges. Many times, we finish our quilts by stitching the front (already quilted) and back right sides together, then turning the right side out. Before turning the quilt, we always trim the edges to keep the bulk down. We often add a few quilting lines through the entire quilt to add that extra bit of stability and texture.

Printing Text

Printing text onto a quilt is not usually a basic step in quilt-making. However, we used some form of printing on the front side of six of our quilts (and on many of the quilt backs), so we have some suggestions for ways to print on material.

- You can hand- or machine-stitch text. For machine-stitching, one method is to set your stitch length to zero, reduce the pressure on the foot of your machine, hold the fabric tightly and move it in a free-form manner. This technique lends itself to script writing (as opposed to printing). You can lay out the writing ahead of time with pencil or chalk. Also, you can usually buy a quilting or darning foot for your machine that is designed specifically for free-motion stitching.
- You can hand- or machine-embroider text. We don't have a sewing machine that embroiders, but many of the new machines do have this capability.
- You can use an indelible fabric marker to write directly onto non-synthetic fabric. Use a light-colored fabric so that the writing will stand out, or use a darker fabric if you wish to create a subtle effect. Set the writing by ironing. You can also use fabric paints in the same way.
- If you have access to a computer and an ink jet printer, you can buy special paper, which will allow you to create iron-on transfers. Use the instructions supplied with the paper. While this technique can produce some terrific printing, you should be forewarned that the result can be a little stiff and shiny and may not be as durable as other printing techniques when it comes to machine washing.
- You can have a photocopy made of your writing and then transfer it onto fabric using acetone. You'll need to go to a copy center and ask them to make the photocopy in a mirror image. Cut out the text and tape it face-down onto the fabric (it should be well-ironed cotton). With a cotton ball or sponge, wipe acetone across the back of the paper, soaking it through. Burnish the image onto the fabric using a stainless steel spoon. Wash the fabric before using it in your quilt. The whole process works better if you transfer the words within a few hours of photocopying. Note: Acetone can be a dangerous substance, so be sure to read, and heed, the manufacturer's warning.

Techniques

On occasion, people have asked us in amazement, "How did you do that?" While our work is innovative and funky, it's not magic. However, there are certain unconventional techniques that we tend to use, and we describe them in the following sections. Within our quilt instructions, you are often referred back to these sections. These techniques are not difficult, and, before long, you'll see how easy it is to do the things we do.

Curved Seam Piecing

We often use the natural world around us as the subject of our quilting: rivers, clouds, hills, etc. These subjects tend to have irregular shapes. Rather than using stiff, straight-lined geometrical patterns to create these things, we use curved-line patterns. Traditional quilting often uses appliqué for irregular-shaped objects, but more often than not we prefer to piece such curved shapes.

For example, take a look at the big rays of the sun in **Night and Day** (page 22). The face of the ray is made up of two pieces of fabric, which meet in a wavy seam down the center of the ray. This is how that seam is pieced together:

1

Make a wavy cut in one piece of material. Use this wavy line as a guide to mark a matching line on the top of the second piece of material. You can mark this edge with pins or with chalk. If you use pencil, it will turn up on the finished top, and you will have to wash it out.

Cut a wavy line into a piece of fabric.

Use the wavy line to lightly mark a second piece of fabric.

2

Now mark a second line ½" beyond the first. This time you can mark the line in pencil if you wish (the reason why you couldn't mark this line right away is because in Step 1 the other piece of material was in the way). Now cut along this second wavy line. Make matching marks with chalk or tiny clips in the seam allowance. You now have two matching pieces ready to sew together.

Mark a second line offset by ½". Cut along this line.

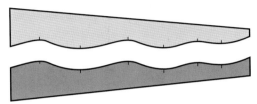

Erase the light line and make tick marks on both pieces of fabric to match the crests and troughs.

3

Set the pieces right sides together, roughly matching the wavy line. You can't match the edges exactly, and that's the problem, or trick, with curved seams. Wherever the two pieces of material cross each other, pin as shown. Stitch the two pieces together with a ¼" seam allowance. As you stitch along, force the two edges to match. This will often cause the rest of the material to buckle. That's okay. Keep the seam edges evenly matched between the pins and/or matching marks, stretching either piece when necessary to prevent puckering. When you get to the end of the seam, clip the curves, open up the piece and press it flat.

Put right sides together and pin where the wavy lines intersect. Stitch along the wavy edge, forcing it to match the drawn line and the tick marks.

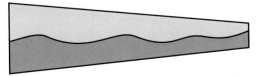

Trim the seam, clip the curves, open and press flat. You now have a curved seam.

If at first things don't come out perfectly flat, don't worry about it too much. A little ironing will often correct or cover this. Actually, we appreciate some of this non-flatness. We think it adds to our quilts. We should also point out that this technique works better with smooth, gentle curves.

Look again at the **Night and Day** quilt. The entire sky is pieced with curved seams. For the sky we did something slightly different. Imagine that we have the sky partly finished, and that we are about to add a new piece. We cut a curve in this new piece and use it to mark our first and second lines onto the already completed sky. After we mark the second line, we don't cut. We just use that line as a guide, i.e., we match the raw edge of our new piece with this marked line. After the new piece is in place, we go back and trim the seams. This is in line with our "piece first, cut second" strategy (see "Cutting and Piecing," page 57).

Other quilts in which we used curved seam piecing include: **Life Is Sweeping Through the Spaces** (page 10); **Playland** (page 16); **Wee Bairn** (page 26); and **Bunnies in the Garden** (page 50).

Inverse Batt Stitching

You know, we use this technique a lot, but we never did come up with a better name for it.

Take the sun ray example once again from **Night and Day** (page 22). Most people who sew will realize that the seam running up the middle of the ray is tricky but that the edge of the ray is easy to achieve. The edge is made by pinning the front and back of the ray right sides together. Even though the edge is curved, the curves of the front and back piece match each other, so it's not too hard to stitch them together with the standard ¼" seam allowance. Once the seam is in place, clip the curves and turn the piece right side out.

So far, we've created a flat sun's ray. Often we want to include batting in these shapes to give them some substance, some depth. Usually this would be done by stuffing in some batting after the piece is turned right side out. We, on the other hand, sew the batting into the ray as we sew the pieces together.

1

Set down some batting, then lay on top of it the front and back of the sun's ray, right sides together. Pin this sandwich to hold it in place.

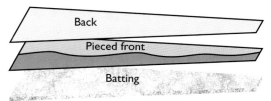

Make a sandwich of the back and front right sides together with batting underneath.

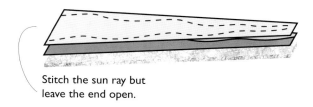

Stitch the sun ray but leave the end open.

2

Stitch along the edge, trim the seams, clip the curves and turn the piece right side out.

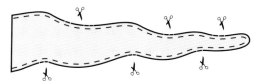

Trim the seam allowances. Clip the inside curves.

Turn the sun ray right side out and press flat.

We call this **inverse batt stitching**. The word **inverse** comes from the fact that the batting starts on the outside rather than on the inside, where it traditionally belongs. The word **batt** comes from the fact that the batting is sewn in.

So what's the difference between the standard technique of adding batting after the piece is turned right side out and inverse batt stitching? In inverse batt stitching, the batting is held in the seams, and it's not going to move around. The batting is also perfectly distributed, even in little nooks and crannies. Lastly, the whole process is simpler. This last point may sound like an exaggeration, but check out **Stay Warm, Stay Well** (page 8), and you'll see how tough it would be to stuff the panels after stitching the side seams.

As we mentioned earlier, we have had no problems running the batting along the feed dogs while stitching (see "Quilting and Finishing," page 58). We suggest that you test out the technique on a small sample first, especially if you are using a softer or looser batt.

As usual, when you stitch right sides together, you will need to have some sort of opening in order to turn the piece right side out. This is true whether or not you include batting. This opening can be made along the seam edge or it can be cut afterwards as a slit on the back. Consider, though, that when using inverse batt stitching, the piece will be bulkier to turn.

One final point. If the finished piece has a front and a back, place the front against the batting and the back on top when laying it out for stitching. This way, the front will look fuller.

Other quilts in which we used inverse batt stitching include: **Life Is Sweeping Through the Spaces** (page 10); **Wee Bairn** (page 26); **Tangible** (page 32); **Classic Theater** (page 40); **Budding Poet** (page 46); and **Bunnies in the Garden** (page 50).

Inset Frames

We discovered this next technique while working on **Night and Day** (page 22). We were looking for an interesting way to make craters in the moon. We thought of trying to simply quilt in circles, but we really wanted the craters to be recessed or inset a bit. Our solution was what we now refer to as an **inset frame**. This is how we did it:

1

Take a piece of material that is at least ½" larger than the crater that you wish to make and set it right side down onto the front of the moon. Pin it in place and draw the crater circle onto the scrap. Stitch around the circle. Cut out the center of the circle, leaving a ¼" seam allowance. Clip the curve, then push the scrap through the hole to the inside, press and… suddenly you have a beautifully finished hole!

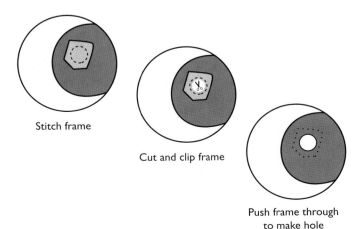

Stitch frame

Cut and clip frame

Push frame through
to make hole

Take a moment to admire your hole. We used plain holes like this in our **Fish on Fridays** trivets/pot holders (page 38).

We refer to the scrap of material used to make the hole as the **frame**. It's always best to choose a material for the frame that is stretchy, because it makes a much cleaner-looking hole.

2

Place another piece of material behind the frame so that it covers the bottom of the hole. We'll refer to this piece as the **bottom**. The next step is to pin the frame to the bottom. Notice that you can lift the front out of the way in order to pin only the frame and the bottom together. Stitch the frame to the bottom using a ¼" seam allowance, and you have a completed crater in which none of the stitching is exposed.

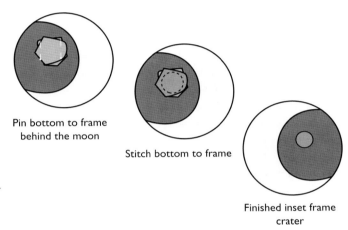

Pin bottom to frame
behind the moon

Stitch bottom to frame

Finished inset frame
crater

This technique has some aesthetic charm for us. It's quite versatile, and we've used it in different manifestations in different quilts. Here are some examples:

- **Playland** (page 16) – holes in making the tunnels.
- **Windsocks** (page 20) – circular holes through the backing and batting, with a cheesecloth bottom, allowing air in to fill the windsocks.
- **Wee Bairn** (page 26) – inset framing of the paw prints.
- **Cabin Fever** (page 28) – triangular inset frames for the cribbage board. These frames were topstitched down to allow one piece of material to function as the bottom for five frames.
- **Baby Bear Hug** (page 34) – diamond-shaped inset frames in the mitts to showcase the tiny bearpaw blocks.
- **Classic Theater** (page 40) – inset framing to make a rectangular hole for the theater stage.
- **Bunnies in the Garden** (page 50) – inset framing to make the many holes for the vegetables, bunnies, etc.

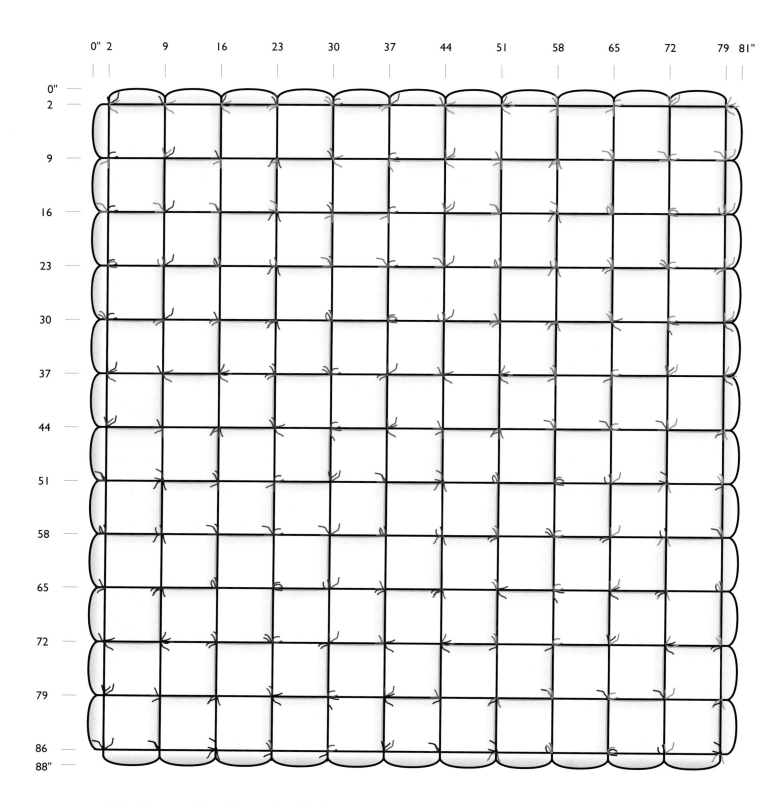

Main Diagram - **Stay Warm, Stay Well**

STAY WARM, STAY WELL

(from page 8)
Quilt Size: 81" x 88"

In this quilt, long panels of simple unbleached cotton are woven together. Panels are tied at the intersections with colorful embroidery cotton or yarn. The border of the quilt is a tube of stuffed unbleached cotton tied off in the same fashion. The design is very simple.

Materials & Cutting

Material	Amount	Use
Unbleached Cotton	22 of 7½" x 85"	11 vertical panels
Unbleached Cotton	24 of 7½" x 78"	12 horizontal panels
Unbleached Cotton	2 of 7½" x 92"	vertical border
Unbleached Cotton	2 of 7½" x 85"	horizontal border
7-oz Batting	3 of 60" x 85"	
Embroidery Cotton	25 skeins	to tie the panels together

TOTAL Unbleached Cotton = 16 yd (60" width) / 15m (150 cm width)

In the Materials & Cutting table above, we have provided the panel sizes required for working on each panel individually. We, however, used lengths of unbleached cotton, stitched the panels first and then cut them after (see Figure 1). This gave us nice straight seams and narrow seam allowances.

Piecing

1

Inverse batt stitch (see "Inverse Batt Stitching," pages 60) each of the panels, leaving one end of each panel open. Turn the panels right side out and press flat. Finish the open ends of the panels with hand-stitching or a machine straight stitch. The finished width is 7" and lengths should be 77" for the horizontal panels and 84" for the vertical panels.

2

Take one of the border pieces and fold it in half along its length, matching right sides together. Stitch the long edge together (but leave the ends open) using a ¼" seam allowance. Turn the tube right side out and stuff it with batting scraps. (Hint: We used long scrap pieces of batting from previous trimmings and stuffed the tube as it was being turned.) Repeat for the other three border pieces. Note: The border pieces are meant to be longer than the panels because they decrease in length considerably when they are tied on.

This quilt has a lot of fabric in it. It is double-thick and therefore contains double the material of your average quilt.

Inverse batt stitch first.

Leave this edge open for turning panels.

Cut out panels after.

(Figure 1)

Finishing

3

Before you weave the panels together, it's a good idea to mark the locations of the ties in order to obtain a uniform weave. These are every 7" along both edges of each panel. We even threaded our embroidery cotton ties into the edges of the panels before weaving them. We used 7" lengths of the full six strands of the embroidery cotton.

4

Lay out all of the horizontal panels side by side. Weave the vertical panels into place. At each of the intersections you will now have four ties (see Figure 2). Working from the center of the quilt out, tie each intersection tightly. Our suggestion is to use a reef knot and add a drop of glue (non-water soluble) or Fray Check™ to the center of the knot afterwards. The glue will help to keep the knot from slipping, because embroidery cotton is slithery stuff.

5

Tie the woven panels together along the edges of the quilt. Use the tails of the embroidery cotton to tie around the border tube, cinching it tight. Start from the center and work your way out to the corners of the quilt. Stitch the ends of the tubes closed. Add two fish, and you're done.

Your Quilt

We decided to start the book with a simple quilt that has a lot of potential for individuality. For your quilt, you could vary the size of the quilt or the width of the panels. You could add variations to the weaving pattern. You could introduce a lot more color by using colored/printed cottons rather than unbleached cotton. You could piece together prints and then make the panels, although you should remember that only half of each panel is exposed to view (and we personally would find it hard to cover up beautiful piecing work). Finally, you could add quilting to the panels before you weave them.

However you choose to make this quilt, you will end up with a deep, warm textured covering.

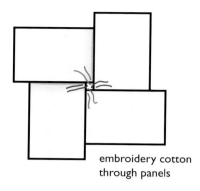

embroidery cotton
through panels

reef knot good

granny knot bad

(Figure 2)

LIFE IS SWEEPING
THROUGH THE SPACES

(from page 10)
Quilt Size: 60" x 80"

One of the beautiful things about this quilt is that you get to start from a work of art. For our quilt, we were inspired by the art of Emily Carr, an amazing artist who lived and worked in the forests of the Pacific Northwest. We took a book out of the library that featured her artwork and used it to draw our own design. Hidden within the quilt is a quote of Emily Carr's, taken from her journals, *Hundreds and Thousands*.

This quilt is one of three in the book that have very flowing designs. For us, there was never an exact pattern that we followed or an explicit end goal. We sketched out our ideas and, to a certain extent, we let the project lead us.

Materials & Cutting

Material	Amount	Use
Various Fabrics	40 pieces	to make the pretty picture
Unbleached Cotton	2 of 60" x 80"	1 for backing, 1 for foundation
	6 of 4" x 12"	for the quote
Brushed Cotton	4 of 4" x 80"	for the border
7-oz Batting	2 of 60" x 80"	to make the quilt cozy-warm
	40" x 80"	for filling the tree, the mountains and the cloud

TOTAL Unbleached Cotton = 6 yd (60" width) / 5.5 m (150 cm width)

The first line of the Materials & Cutting table is pretty vague. What we did was draw out our design onto one of the (prewashed) lengths of unbleached cotton. This foundation was used to help lay out and piece the design. For our quilt, the "various fabrics" came from second-hand clothing. The quote contained within the quilt is hidden under buttoned enclosures, so we used old shirts with buttons that we liked for this purpose.

Piecing

Use a soft-leaded pencil or a fabric marker to sketch the artwork onto one of the sheets of unbleached cotton. These lines will be used as a rough guide in the piecing of the quilt. If necessary, draw the grid lines on first. The grid lines can be used to reduce or enlarge the size of the quilt.

At this stage you can also prepare the quote (see "Printing Text," page 58, for ideas about printing on fabric). We handwrote the quote using an indelible marker on the six 4" x 12" pieces of unbleached cotton.

Draw the design onto a foundation sheet of fabric. Start piecing one row at a time.

Piece the rows together first and then stitch the row onto the foundation. Stitch the first line of the quote behind a buttoned piece of fabric ahead of time.

(Figure 1)

1

Piecing the Sky   Picture the sky as a series of rows along the lines you have drawn; the cutting and piecing happens one row at a time (see Figure 1). Stitch the sky directly onto the foundation of unbleached cotton. For an explanation of how to piece in this fashion, see "Curved Seam Piecing" (page 59).

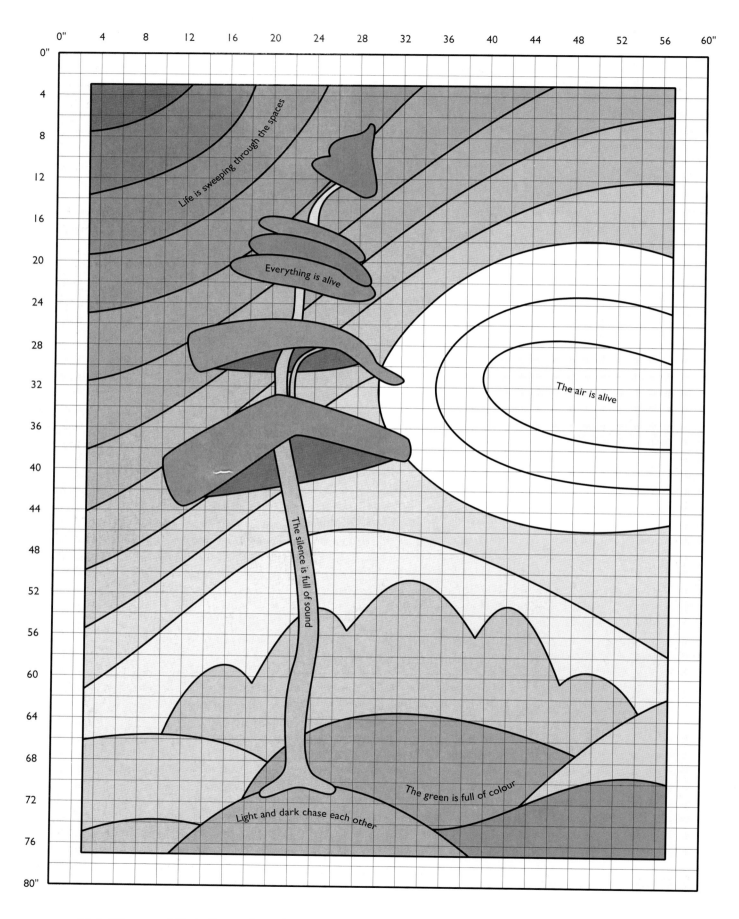

Main Diagram - **Life Is Sweeping Through the Spaces**

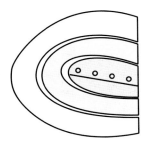

Put the third line of the quote in place. Piece the cloud from the center out.

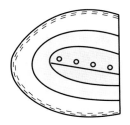

Put in a double baste along the edge of the cloud and gather. Turn the edge under and topstitch the cloud into the sky.

(Figure 2)

Layer the mountain backing, the mountain front and some batting.

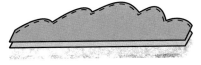

Inverse batt stitch along the top edge. Clip curves and turn right sides out.

Stitch the mountains to the quilt front 2" from the top. This leaves a little valley behind.

(Figure 3)

Start in the top left corner with your darkest blue material and make your way toward the cloud and the mountains. Don't worry too much about the outside edges of the quilt because, in the end, the border will cover them. When you come to a row with more than one piece in it, first stitch the pieces together and then, using curved seam piecing, stitch the row onto the foundation as a single piece. The first line of the quote goes behind one of the first few rows of sky. Use a piece of material with a row of buttons (e.g., a dark blue shirt). Center the quote behind the buttons and stitch in place, then continue piecing the row. Continue with the sky until it's finished. There is no need to piece the area under the cloud.

2

Piecing the Cloud Stitch together the rows of the cloud with the third line of the quote before piecing the cloud onto the foundation (see Figure 2). Start with the center piece of material and the quote. Once again, use curved seam piecing. Although the first stitching line has a tight "U" shape, curved seam piecing will still work. Add rows around the center piece until you have a cloud that is a little larger than the space where it will go in the sky. We made our cloud about 2" bigger all the way around. Don't try to be too exact with the size and shape of the cloud; just make sure that it is bigger than the area it will cover.

3

Baste two rows around the edge of the cloud, which will be used to gather the material (gathering the cloud will make it fluffier in appearance). Pull the gathering stitches until the cloud is the right size for the opening in the sky. Turn the edges of the cloud under (including the gather), then place a layer of batting under the cloud and topstitch it into place.

4

Piecing the Mountains and Hills The mountains are made to stand out from the sky by having a little valley behind them. Choose or piece the material for the front and back of the mountains and make an inverse batt sandwich (see "Inverse Batt Stitching," page 60), as shown in Figure 3. Stitch the shape of the mountains, trim the seams, clip the curves, turn right side out and press flat.

Use chalk to mark a line 2" below the top edge of the mountains. Pin the mountains in place so that the chalked line will cover the raw edges of the pieced sky and the valley. Stitch on the mountains along the chalked line so that there is a 2" valley behind.

5

The hills are pieced onto the foundation in the same way as the sky. Two more lines of the quote go in under the hills. Wow, nice job.

6

Piecing the Tree The tree is made up of four green branches and four pieces of trunk. The two upper branches sit in front of the tree trunk. The two lower branches appear to wrap around the trunk. Make the two upper branches using the inverse batt stitch technique (see Figure 4). Cut a slit in the back of the upper branches and turn them right side out through the slit. Notice that there's another piece of the quote in the second set of branches.

7

For the two lower branches, begin with the inverse batt stitch technique (as in Step 6). Now choose a matching piece of material in a slightly darker shade of green. Cut to shape and hand-stitch it onto the back of the branches folding in the raw edge as you stitch. Finish the raw bottom edge by folding it under and machine- or hand-stitching. This will make a pocket for the trunk.

8

The trunk pieces are cut long to tuck under the branches, but in width they are cut without a seam allowance. We placed another line of the quote behind a salvaged zipper in the trunk. Set the tree aside until most of the quilting is complete (Step 11). We stitched continuous quilting lines in behind the tree to make it stand right out.

Quilting

9

Lay out the two sheets of batting. Set the front of the quilt right side up on top of the batting. Pin or baste the layers together. The distance between the quilting lines will vary because the rows of the sky are not a consistent width. In our example, the quilting lines are 1½" to 3" apart. Quilt along the seams of the rows in the sky and in the cloud, as well as inside the rows, in order to get the desired spacing of lines.

Note: Don't quilt through the quotes! Pay special attention to the buttoned areas to make sure that you can still unfasten them and read the quotes.

10

Quilt the first line of the mountains along the chalk line marked 2" from the top. Quilt in concentric lines down to the hills. Similarly, quilt along the seam of each hill and then in concentric lines to cover each hill.

11

Now that most of the quilting is done, attach the tree to the front of the quilt before the back goes on. Attach the top two sections of the trunk. The trunk pieces are attached to the quilt using a satin stitch along the edge. Hand-stitch the top branch of the tree. Machine- or hand-stitch the second and third branches. Satin-stitch the third section of the trunk, starting right up in the pocket of the third branch. Attach the lowest branch and lowest section of the trunk in the same fashion.

Finishing

12

Because of the piecing and the deep quilting, the quilt will no longer be nice and square. Trim the edges to make it square again. Pin or baste the backing onto the quilt, making the traditional quilt sandwich.

13

Start with one of the side border pieces – the 4" strips of flannel. Set it right side down on top of the quilt, 3" from the trimmed edge, and pin it in place. Stitch the border piece down along its outside edge. Press the border outwards so that it extends ¾" beyond the trimmed edge. The extra-large seam allowance makes it easy to finish the quilt. Attach the other three border pieces in the same way.

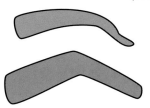

Make the branches using Inverse Batt Stitching.

This second set of branches has a quote behind it.

Begin the lower branches in the same way - with an Inverse Batt Stitch.

Finish the lower branches with a piece of darker fabric hand stitched behind. Stitch along the dotted line only. This creates a pocket for the tree trunk, with the branches wrapping around.

(Figure 4)

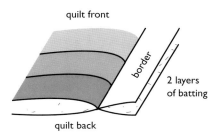

quilt front

border

2 layers
of batting

quilt back

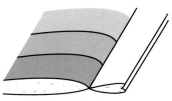

wrap border and backing
between 2 layers of batting

stitch, catching border,
backing & wrap

(Figure 5)

14

Wrap the backing and the border around and in between the two layers of quilt batting and pin in place (see Figure 5). Run a continuous stitch around the edge of the quilt.

15

Quilt over just a few of the major quilting lines in order to secure the backing. By now the quilt is big, so working with it in a machine can be pretty tough. Don't quilt through the tree. To finish the quilt off, add two fish ... maybe as buttons in the cloud.

Your Quilt

For this quilt, you could start with an entirely different design. Other genres of art that would be suitable for a quilt such as this one are Impressionism (Vincent Van Gogh), Fauvism (Henri Matisse), Cubism (Pablo Picasso), abstract art (lots) and pop art (Andy Warhol). Another beautiful art form that is well suited to this project is Aboriginal art. Or you could forego genres of art altogether and use a vista of nature that takes your breath away.

Whether you choose to work from our design, a different work of art or something entirely of your own creation, it is important to keep the lines relatively simple and flowing. Draw your design onto a piece of graph paper just as we did, and stitch away.

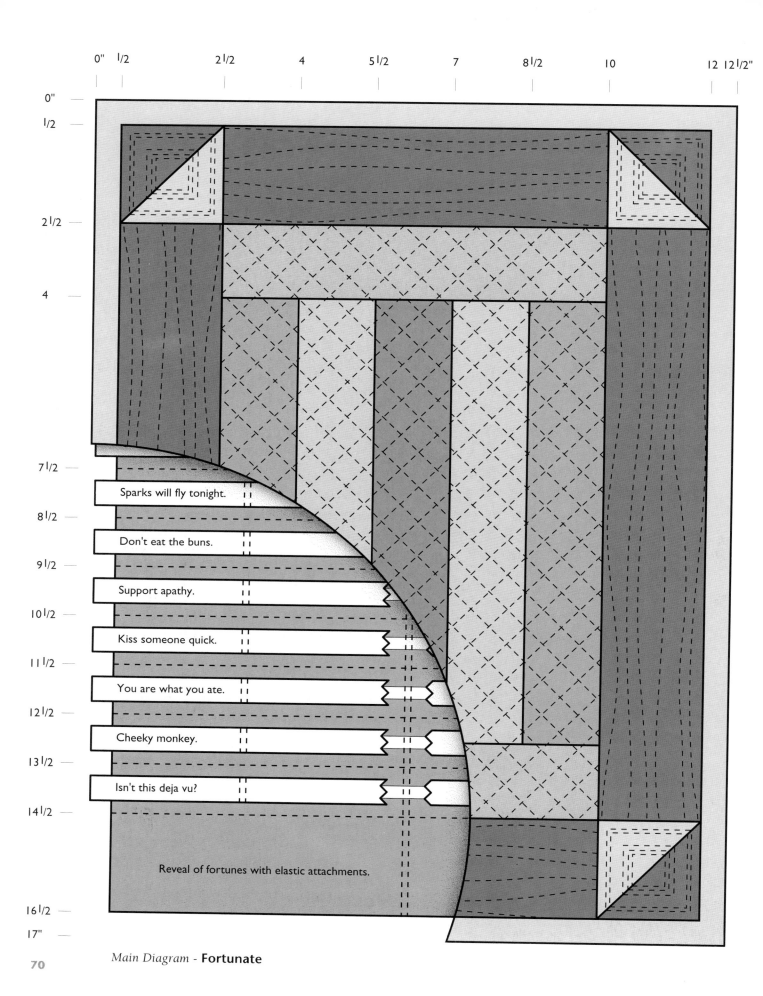

Sparks will fly tonight.

Don't eat the buns.

Support apathy.

Kiss someone quick.

You are what you ate.

Cheeky monkey.

Isn't this deja vu?

Reveal of fortunes with elastic attachments.

Main Diagram - **Fortunate**

FORTUNATE

(from page 14)
Placemat Size: 12½" x 17"

These placemat tops were inspired by a quilt featured in a beautiful book called *Amish Quilts of Lancaster County* by Julie Silber (Esprit de Corps, 1990). Using this very quilt as inspiration, we duplicated the pattern but changed the red in the color scheme to purple and added a bit of quilting around the edges. The bars design and the diamond quilting pattern were both common in Lancaster County Amish quilts.

In these quilted placemats, fortunes are printed on unbleached cotton tabs, which hide inside the placemats and can be pulled out at the end of each meal. The fortunes are attached to elastic, so they slip back into place once they have been read.

Materials & Cutting (for four placemats)

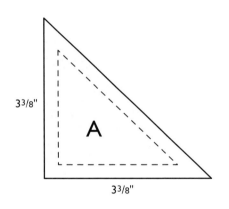

3³⁄₈"

A

3³⁄₈"

(Figure 1)

Material	Amount	Use
Purple	8 of 2½" x 8"	outside borders
	8 of 2½" x 12½"	outside borders
	4 of 12" x 16½"	backing
Turquoise	8 of 2" x 9½"	inside bars
Brown	4 of 2" x 9½"	inside bars (center)
Green	8 of 2" x 9½"	inside bars
	16 triangles A	front corners
Gray	8 of 2" x 8"	vertical rectangles
Gold	8 of 1" x 16½"	binding
	8 of 1" x 13"	binding
	16 triangles A	front corners
Satin	4 of 13" x 17½"	lining for fronts
Satin	4 of 12" x 16½"	lining for backs
Polar Fleece™	4 of 13" x 17½"	batting replacement
Unbleached Cotton	2 of 12½" x 48"	fortunes
Elastic	40' of ³⁄₈" wide	pulling out fortunes

The fabrics were (once again) salvaged from old clothes and finished (but no longer used) projects. They include linen, both lightweight and heavier cottons and rayon.

Piecing

1

Placemats   Using a ¼" seam allowance, piece together each of the four placemat tops. Start with the center bars and bar ends, then stitch the long purple outside borders to the center block. Next, sew pieced corner blocks to the shorter purple outside borders. Stitch these two edge strips to the middle section. Press all seams.

2

Fortunes   To assemble the fortunes, start by marking lines 1" apart on one of your pieces of unbleached cotton. Place the second piece of unbleached cotton underneath, and stitch 48 rectangles, 12" long, using your drawn lines as a guide for the sewing machine foot. After cutting along the lines, you will end up with ½" wide rectangles (see Figure 2). Using pinking shears, cut all of the rectangles in half, clip the corners and turn right side out. This will make 96 fortunes; 24 for each placemat. Iron flat.

3

For various options for printing the fortunes onto the finished rectangles, see "Printing Text" (page 58). We had access to a computer, so we printed out a mirror-image of all the fortunes and then used iron-on transfer paper to transfer the printing directly onto the fabric. Whatever method you use, make certain that the printing is permanent, as you will likely want to wash your placemats fairly frequently. When printing onto the fabric, leave a ½" space at the beginning and end of each fortune. This gives the fortune puller a little more space to grip onto the material without covering any words, and it keeps the fortunes completely hidden (so they can't be read by simply lifting the edge of the placemat).

4

Use a 10" piece of elastic and slip a fortune rectangle onto each end. Push the elastic into the fortunes until the casings are ½" apart. Stitch the elastic in place ¼" below the printing (see Figure 3). Make sure this stitch is strong, because this is what holds the fortunes securely inside the placemat.

Quilting

5

A batting of thin Polar Fleece™ was used instead of polyester batting for ease of quilting and so that the placemat would remain flat. Stitch the placemat top onto the Polar Fleece™ in order to keep the whole placemat square. Quilt through the placemat top and Polar Fleece™ only.

Quilt the center block of rectangles first. We chose to quilt the traditional Amish diagonal diamond pattern, using the sewing machine foot as a guide to line up all of the stitching (so the stitching is ¼" apart). The quilting in the purple sections consists of random wavy lines, about nine lines per section (to keep the stitching density similar throughout). The corners have a square pattern, which is fairly closely stitched (see Main Diagram for quilting lines).

Finishing

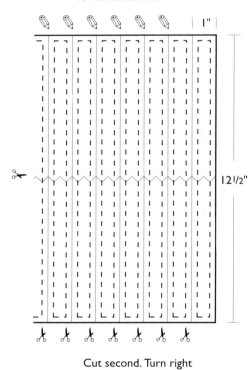

Mark lines with pencil & stitch rectanges (x 48) for fortunes first.

Cut second. Turn right sides out and press flat.

(Figure 2)

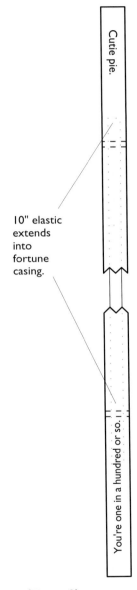

Satin lining was used so that the fortunes, once pulled out, would slip easily back into position.

Cutie pie.

10" elastic extends into fortune casing.

You're one in a hundred or so.

(Figure 3)

6

With right sides together, pin a satin lining to each of the four backs of the placemats. Stitch around each rectangle, leaving an opening on one side. Turn right side out and press. Close all openings with hand-stitching.

7

On the satin side of each of the four finished back pieces, place 12 of the fortune pairs as shown in the main diagram. When in place, sew two lines across the center of the backing to catch all of the elastics without catching the fortune casings. Again, these stitch lines must be fairly solid.

8

Place the four remaining satin rectangles on top of the fortunes (satin side in). Sew between adjacent fortunes. This will create a channel for each fortune.

For each placemat pin the top and back right sides together (see Figure 4). Stitch the front and the second satin lining together, careful to avoid catching the tips of the fortunes. Leave an opening on one side, turn and finish by handstitching.

Your Quilt

If you choose a different design for your placemat, it is important that you use a pattern that is symmetric (so you can't tell the top from the bottom), and you will need to make sure that every placemat looks the same. This way none of the fortunes are "marked" by their location.

Many of the fortunes we used were written by friends at a dinner party, but there are many other sources that you can try. One easy way to come up with fortunes is to buy a box of fortune cookies (or do a lot of eating out at Chinese restaurants!). Another source is, believe it or not, the Internet (just use the phrase **fortune cookies** in your search engine). And, of course, you could write them yourself. After all, the more personal your fortunes are, the more fun they will be for your guests.

Satin lining with fortunes in channels underneath

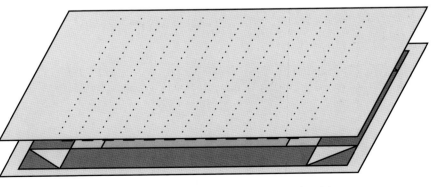

(Figure 4)

Pieced front, right side up

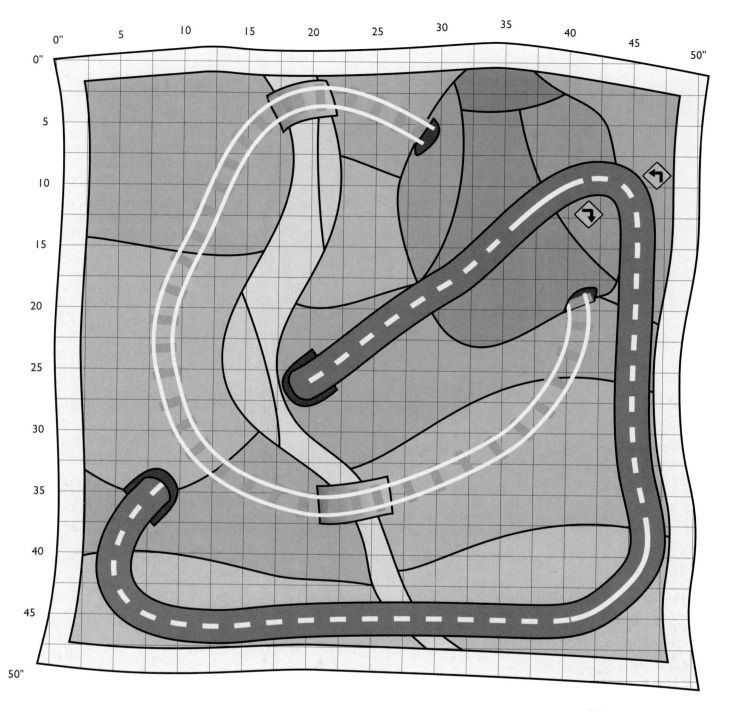

Main Diagram

PLAYLAND

(from page 16)
Quilt Size: 50" x 50"

This quilt was designed as a mat for playing on. The landscape elements include fields, a river, a hill, a road, road signs, train tracks, tunnels and bridges. The actual layout of the landscape and the elements within it can be altered very easily to suit your own ideas. We've also included the option of an attached duffel bag, which the mat can be rolled into and carried away to a new destination.

Materials & Cutting

Material	Amount	Use
Unbleached Cotton	1 of 48" x 48"	foundation for piecing on the landscape
	1 of 50" x 50"	quilt backing
	4 of 2½" x 50"	front border
Various Fabrics	30 pieces	greens, browns & blues for river & fields
Black Terry Cloth	3½" x 100"	highway
Black Broadcloth	3½" x 100"	highway backing
Yellow Polar Fleece™		"painted" highway lines
Silver Seam Bias Binding	200" of ¼" wide	railway track
Brown Corduroy	20" x 20"	railway ties
Black Stretchy Denim	4 of 4" x 4"	tunnels (stretchy so that hands can go through easily)
	2 of 12" x 20"	
Batting	50" x 50"	the quilt
	various pieces	to fill the hill
Heavy Cotton – Plaid	25½" x 45"	duffel bag*
Heavy Cotton – Blue	14" circle	duffel bag end
Heavy Cotton – Green	14" circle	duffel bag end
Separating Zipper	24"	
Webbing and Plastic Clips		duffel bag strap

*Note: Don't cut the duffel bag piece until you've completed the quilt and checked its size when rolled up. The size of your quilt will depend on whether you used more or less batting than we did, and the size of your duffel bag can be adjusted accordingly.

If you want, give the river some perspective by widening it at one end.

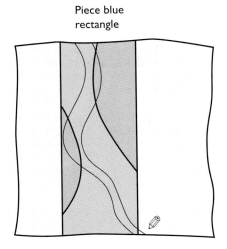

Piece blue rectangle

Draw on river

(Figure 1)

Piecing

1

River   Begin with the river by piecing the blues together to form a large rectangle, approximately 20" x 48' (see Figure 1). Stitch the rectangle down onto the 48" x 48" foundation of unbleached cotton. Use a soft-leaded pencil to draw the meandering river shape onto the blue rectangle.

2

Green Fields   The green fields are first pieced as a large square, approximately 48" x 48" in size. Cut the fields into two halves to match the river's edge drawn in pencil. See Figure 2. Cut two pieces of batting to match the field shapes, but add an additional 2" to the outside edges so that it extends beyond the quilt (the borders will cover this in the end). Place the field and backing right sides together with the batting on top, match curves and inverse batt stitch along the river's edge (see "Inverse Batt Stitching," page 60). Trim seams, clip curves and fold the green fields back overtop the batting. Baste the fields and batting down to the top sheet along the edges to make it more secure.

3

Hill   The hill is pieced in greens and browns and is approximately 20" wide. Piece a circle that is 25" wide. Stitch in darts, to obtain a three-dimensional hill.

4

Train Tunnel The tunnel through the hill needs to be built at this point. It is completed using the inset frame technique (see "Inset Frames," page 61). Draw the tunnel entrance shape (see Figure 3) onto 2 of the 4" denim squares. Pin them to the base of the hill where the tunnel entrance and exit will be (see Main Diagram for placement). Stitch the tunnel entrance shape through the square and the hill fabric, and cut out the inside of the entrance through all layers, about ¼" from the seam line. Flip the black square frame through to the inside.

Construct the tunnel using one of the larger pieces of black denim fabric. Sew train tracks onto the denim piece (see Step 6, "Train Tracks," for more details), then form the tunnel by stitching the long edge, right sides together, so that it forms a tube. Stitch the tube on the inside to the inset frame, right sides together.

5

With the tunnel now completed and in place, stuff the hill loosely with batting, fold its raw edge under ½", place it onto the field and topstitch into place. Leave a small opening at the base of the tunnel entrance/exit holes so that the train rails that run on the rest of the mat can be completed by being tucked beneath the hill.

6

Train Tracks The rest of the train tracks should be laid now. The rails were made of ¼" silver seam binding tape. For the ties, we used scraps of brown corduroy finished to ½" x 2¼". We laid the ties onto the field at 2" intervals, with the rails on top 1¼" apart. Sew along the rails, through the ties and onto the quilt. Finish the tracks by tucking them under the hill and matching them to the tunnel's tracks. After this step is completed, finish your hill with topstitching.

7

The two train bridges that cross the river are finished rectangles of fabric that have the train tracks stitched on top of them. These rectangles are then stitched to the river banks on both sides. This way, boats are able to run underneath the bridges.

8

Road The road is made from 3½" wide black terry cloth strips, with yellow Polar Fleece™ (the "painted" center lines) sewn on top with a satin stitch. Cut black broadcloth strips of the same dimensions to line the road. Stitch the broadcloth and terry cloth right sides together, then turn right side out. Sections of the road were joined together to make the entire length. Where the road curves, cut these pieces out in the curved shape and line as above. Clip corners for curved sections before turning. Lay the road out completely on your mat to ensure that it is the correct length. The ends of the road will join and be finished inside the road tunnel.

9

Road Tunnel Make the tunnel that runs under the river the same way that you made the train tunnel through the hill. Draw the tunnel entrance shape onto two 4" black squares. Place these on either side of the river (see Main Diagram for placement), stitch down through all layers and cut out the inside of the entrance shape. Flip the black pieces through to the back. Cut and finish the tunnel tube piece as in Step 4 (the only difference here is that the road is not sewn into the tunnel tube but is left loose). Finish the empty tube and stitch it to the tunnel entrance/exit holes as in Step 4.

76

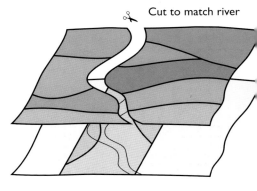

Piece green fields

Cut to match river

(Figure 2)

Note: Make an extra 28" of straight road to use on the duffel bag.

Frame for tunnel
entrances

Stitch tracks onto tunnel rectangle

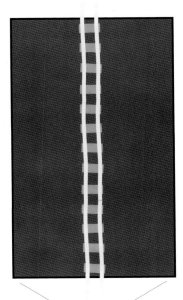

After, match these two edges together
to make the tunnel tube

(Figure 3)

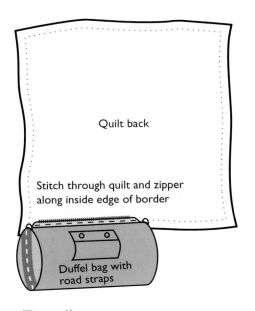

(Figure 4)

*Fill the bag's pocket with cars and
trains (and two fish), and you're all set!*

10

Feed the road through the road tunnel. Hand-stitch the two ends of the road together. Push the road back through the tunnel so that it is properly set in place (with the joined seam close to the center of the tunnel). Working from the tunnel entrance/exit holes, stitch the road onto the mat along each road edge, leaving it unstitched over the hill and over the river.

11

Road Signs Make the road signs from scraps of gold corduroy, with the arrows embroidered on by hand or satin-stitched by machine (you could also use fabric paint). The signs are sewn onto the mat by hand at both locations.

Finishing

12

Stitch the border to the edges of the top of the quilt, fold out and press. With right sides together, stitch the quilt backing to the mat, leaving a 12" opening on one side where the duffel bag will join. Turn right side out and press. Finish the opening with hand stitching. Quilt through all layers of the quilt around the inside edge of the border.

13

Duffel Bag Check the measurement of your quilt folded in half and rolled up. Cut your duffel bag material to fit. To make the duffel bag, first baste the two leftover pieces of road onto the circular pieces at both edges. On the rectangular piece, fold under $\frac{1}{2}$" along the top and bottom narrow edges and stitch one side of the zipper to each of these edges. With some left over scraps, stitch a flat pocket onto the rectangular piece 3" below the top edge.

With right sides together, stitch the circles to the long edges of the rectangle. Sew a webbing strap with clips, which will attach to the road straps for carrying.

14

Unzip the duffel bag, place the bottom edge of the quilt inside the bag and stitch the bag onto the quilt back (see Figure 4). Now you can fold the mat in half, roll it up and stuff it away in the duffel bag.

Your Quilt

You could simplify this quilt by leaving out the duffel bag option for a more permanent "stay and play at home" mat. If you choose not to go with the duffel bag, you could scale the whole mat up to a bed size (as long as you aren't worried about your child staying up all night playing!). The top of this playful quilt can be altered as much as you like to make it more personal – how about a replica of an area that you and your children are familiar with?

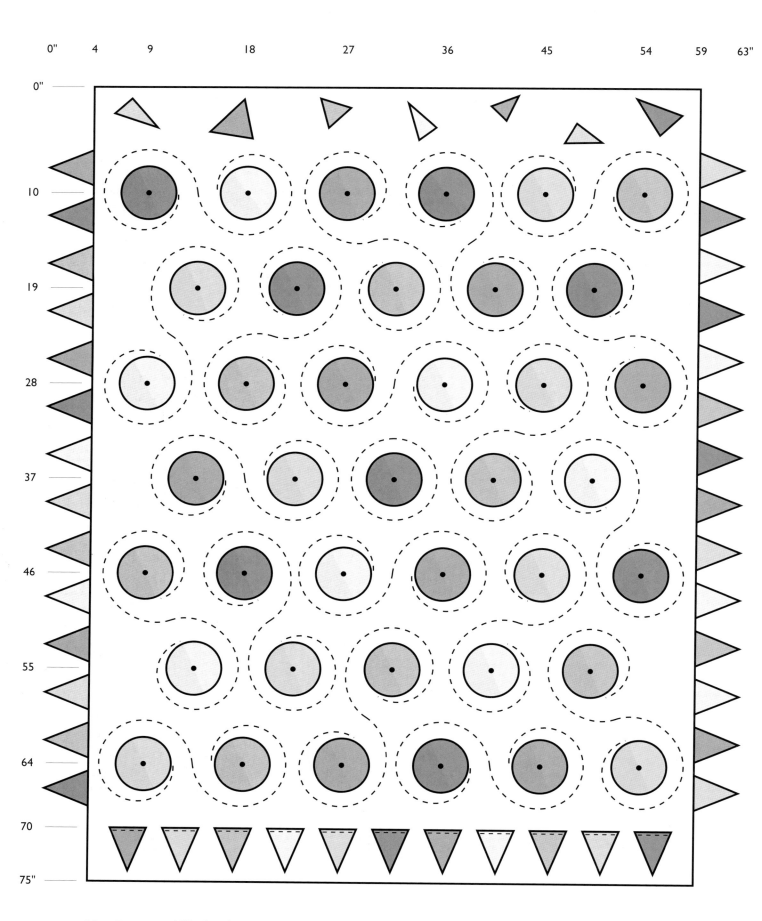

Main Diagram - **Windsocks**

WINDSOCKS

(from page 20)
Quilt Size: 55" x 75"

This fun quilt has colorful cones on it that fill with air and stand up when the quilt is luffed. When we were making this quilt the trick was to try to find a way to get the air into the cones. After extensive testing at the Two Fish labs, the solution was to cut holes through the backing and batting and cover them with cheesecloth. The cheesecloth allows enough air to pass into the cones while still being durable enough to serve as the quilt bottom. As for the cones, the choice of fabric will factor into how well they'll stand at attention – we used 100% cotton, and they are stiff enough to stand up by themselves … with, of course, some luffing.

Materials & Cutting

Material	Amount	Use
Unbleached Cotton	2 of $55\frac{1}{2}$" x $75\frac{1}{2}$"	top and backing
	36" x 42"	cut into 39 6" squares for inset frames
Colored 100% Cotton	5 of 26" x 42"	39 large and 39 small cones
Cheesecloth	36" x 42"	cut into 39 6" squares for covering holes in back
7-oz Batting	$55\frac{1}{2}$" x $75\frac{1}{2}$"	

TOTAL Unbleached Cotton = 8 yd (45" width) / 7 m (110 cm width)
TOTAL Colored Cotton (for each color) = 1.1 yd (45" width) / 1 m (110 cm width)

Piecing

1

Large Cones On the quilt top, mark 39 $4\frac{1}{2}$" diameter circles, placed cookie sheet style, with four rows of six circles and three rows of five circles (see Main Diagram for placement). Mark the first row of circles 10" below the top edge of the sheet (measured to the center of the circles) to allow for some space at the top of the quilt. Cut out the circles.

2

Mark each circle and each cone with $\frac{1}{4}$ markings, as shown on the pattern in Figure 1. Pin together each of the $\frac{1}{4}$ markings and sew the large cone pieces into the circles on the quilt top (right sides together), matching edges and using a $\frac{1}{4}$" seam allowance. Keep the seam smooth by adjusting every inch or so. Make sure that $\frac{1}{4}$" of the cone fabric side seams extends beyond each end of stitching. Sew the cone side seams to complete the cone shape. It is best to make the cones in this sequence, as it is easier to stitch the circular seam first and to complete the cone with a straight stitch after.

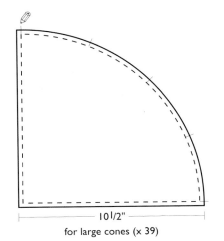

$10\frac{1}{2}$"
for large cones (x 39)

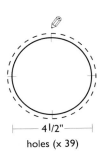

$4\frac{1}{2}$"
holes (x 39)

(Figure 1)

If you don't have a compass to draw circles, then do what we do... search through the house for the right size bowl, cup, tin can, etc.

3

Holes   Make the holes in the back sheet using the inset frame technique (see "Inset Frames," page 61). On the wrong side of each cotton square, draw a 4½" circle. Mark the locations of the holes on the backing to match the cones on the front. Place the cotton squares right side down over the backing and batting. Stitch around the circle with a ¼" seam, then cut out the circle. Clip curves. Flip the square through the hole so that it covers both the backing and batting, then press flat. Place the cheesecloth square into the hole at the back of all layers and topstitch into place through all layers.

4

Small Cones   Stitch the seam of each small cone with right sides together, turn and press flat with the seam running down the back center of each cone (see Figure 2). Trim the bottom edge to complete the triangle shape. Baste cones right sides together along the side edges of the quilt top so that the cones point into the center of the top. For the remaining small cones (along the bottom of the quilt), turn and press raw edges to the inside, then hand or machine-appliqué to the quilt top as shown in the Main Diagram.

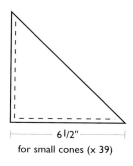

6½"
for small cones (x 39)

(Figure 2)

Quilting and Finishing

5

Place the quilt top and backing right sides together and stitch around all edges, leaving a 10" opening along the bottom edge. Trim seams and turn right side out, finishing the opening with hand-stitching. Be certain that the top and bottom holes are completely aligned before you begin quilting. (This might best be accomplished by basting the layers together first).

6

Complete the quilting by machine-sewing a spiral pattern around pairs of cones (see Main Diagram for quilting line placement).

7

Using leftover scraps of the colored fabric, cut out small triangles (and two fish?), press under ¼" on all sides, then pin and machine-appliqué them through all layers along the top edge of the quilt.

Your Quilt

The most obvious ways to change or personalize this quilt is to vary the colors, the number of cones or the placement of the cones. Another idea would be to attach jingle bells or tassels of yarn to the ends of a few cones. The addition of bells would mean that the cones might not stand up very well, but the luffing of the quilt would be a little more musical!

NIGHT AND DAY

(from page 22)
Quilt Size: 68" x 76"

This fun and friendly night-and-day quilt is a celebration of color. It begins, up top, with a violet sky that progresses to indigo, to blue, then, finally, to off-white at the horizon. The light green peaks of the hills also change, moving into darker shades of green and browns at the bottom of the quilt. The sun presides over this beautiful scene in yellows, oranges, reds and whites. Beneath the sun hides a moon in silver and black. And beside the moon (under the rays of the sun) are tiny little mother-of-pearl stars – natural spectrums all on their own.

The sun is fastened onto the quilt with buttons hidden behind the moon. When the sun is out, the quilt welcomes you with its warmth. When it is "down," the moon makes the night sky appear cool and mysterious.

Materials & Cutting

Material	Amount	Use
Assorted Blue & Purple Scraps	30 pieces	the sky
Assorted Green & Brown Scraps	20 pieces	the land
Assorted Yellow to Red Scraps	20 pieces	the sun
Silver & Black Velvet	20" x 20"	the moon
Star Buttons	20	friends of the moon
Unbleached Cotton	68½" x 76½"	backing
	4 of 6½" x 68½"	border
7-oz Batting	68" x 76"	the quilt
	40" x 60"	filling the sun and moon

TOTAL Unbleached Cotton = 5.2 yd (60" width) / 4.7 m (150 cm width)

Almost all of the pieces of this quilt are odd shapes. You may think it took a lot of careful planning and cutting. It didn't. We began with a general color scheme and then worked with what material we had – most of which, once again, was salvaged from old clothing. For example, look closely and you'll see scraps of used pants with the pockets intact right in the quilt.

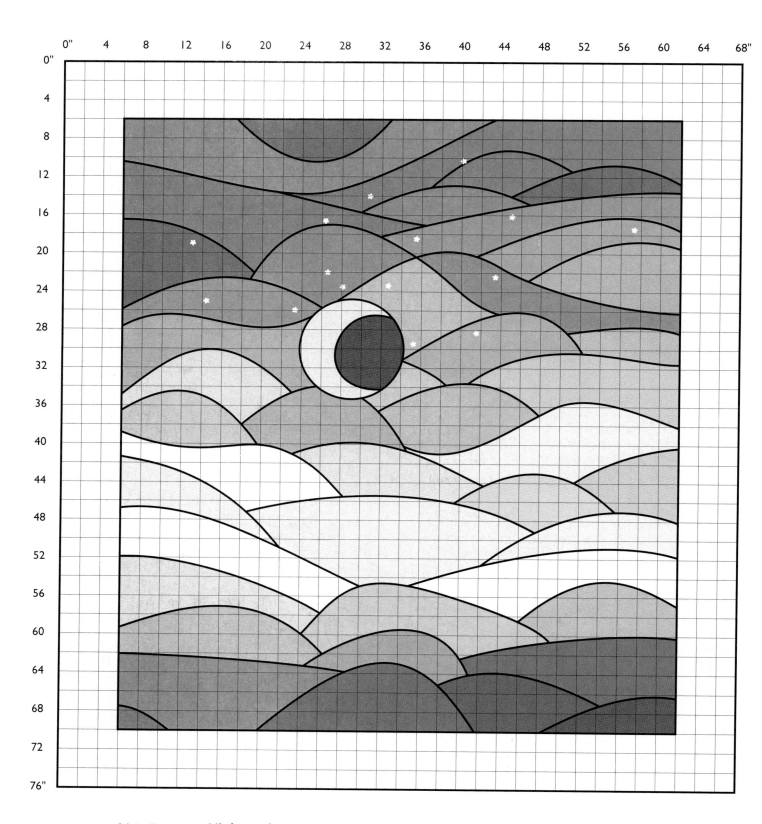

Main Diagram - **Night and Day (moon sky)**

Put inset frame craters into the silver and dark sides of the moon.

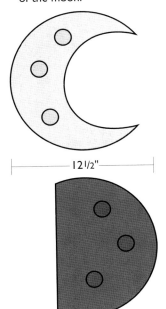

|← 12 1/2" →|

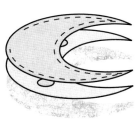

Inverse batt stitch the sides of the moon

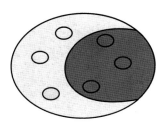

Appliqué the finished pieces to the quilt top.

(Figure 1)

Piecing

1

Piecing the Sky   Start from the top of the sky and work your way down. Use curved seam piecing to build the sky (see "Curved Seam Piecing," page 59). We used our darkest purples at the top and worked our way down to off white. Add to the sky until you have a piece approximately 56 1/2" wide by 45" long.

2

Piecing the Hills   For the hills, work from the horizon to the bottom of the quilt. We used lighter colors at the horizon and progressed to darker colors at the bottom of the quilt. The hills are very similar to the sky, except that we made them three-dimensional. Use the same technique as described for the mountain in **Life Is Sweeping Through the Spaces** (page 67). Repeat for all of the hills, until your pieced front is at least 56 1/2" wide by 64 1/2" long.

3

Piecing the Moon   The moon comes in two pieces: the silver crescent piece and the dark piece (see Figure 1). Both pieces have finished backs, and they are not attached to each other. The moon is able to open up (ssshhhh – don't tell!).

The first step in making the moon is to add some craters to its surface. We describe our technique for adding craters to the moon in "Inset Frames," page 61. We used silver craters on the silver piece of the moon and black craters on the black piece. Next , add the backs to each piece of the moon using an inverse batt stitch. Use a light batting. Stitch around each piece, leaving a small opening. Turn right side out and close openings with hand-stitching.

4

Choose where you would like the sun and moon to sit in the sky. Set the two finished pieces of the moon together (craters facing up) with the silver crescent overlaying the black piece to make an 11" circle. Hand-stitch or appliqué the outside edge of the moon onto the quilt top. This is the finished moon, complete with secret pocket.

5

Piecing the Sun   The cutting and assembly of the sun is illustrated in Figure 2. Start with one of the sun's rays. Cut the two front pieces, then piece them together with curved seam piecing. Cut the back of the ray and some batting. Inverse batt stitch the ray, leaving open the end that attaches to the sun. Turn the ray right side out through this opening. Repeat for the other 15 rays. Note: We made the small rays uniform in size, but for the big rays, we varied the size according to how much material we had.

6

Cut and piece the center of the sun using curved seam piecing. Match the open edges of the rays to the center of the sun, placing right sides together. Pin the rays in place and stitch them to the center of the sun. Note: It might help to do this step twice, first for the small rays and then for the big rays.

7

Cut a backing of sturdy fabric for the center of the sun. Sew a reinforced buttonhole in the center of the backing. Add some batting for the center of the sun, and hand-stitch the backing onto the back of the sun. This is the finished sun, which can be set aside.

8

Piecing the Border   Square the pieced front to measure 56½" wide by 64½" long. Sew the side borders onto the front of the quilt right sides together. Open and press. Repeat for the top and bottom borders.

Quilting

9

Pin the quilt front onto the batting. We used the lines of the piecing to direct our quilting. Start at the top of a piece of the sky and quilt along the seam line. Offset from this line 1" down and quilt again. Continue to echo the quilting at 1" intervals until you have covered the piece. Repeat for all pieces in the sky. Do the same for each hill, but begin 1" down from the tops of the hills so that the little valley remains open. Break quilting across the moon.

Finishing

10

Pin the backing right side down onto the face of the quilt. Stitch around the edge of the quilt using a ¼" seam allowance. Leave a 12" opening at the bottom of the quilt and turn the quilt right side out through this opening. Close the opening with hand-stitching. Stabilize the backing by stitching over a few of the quilting lines in the bottom half of the quilt.

11

Scatter the stars in the night sky. Sew the stars onto the quilt through all layers. Open up the pocket behind the moon and sew a button for the sun into the center of the moon backing. This should be a sturdy button. If it's daytime, button on your sun. Now add two fish, and you're done.

Hint: We placed most of the stars so that they would be hidden by the rays of the sun.

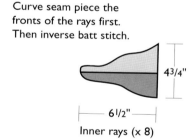

6¼"

5½"

Section of sun center (x 8).
Curve seam piece sun center.

12½"

Curve seam piece the
fronts of the rays first.
Then inverse batt stitch.

4¾"

6½"

Inner rays (x 8)

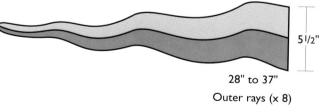

5½"

28" to 37"

Outer rays (x 8)

(Figure 2)

Your Quilt

At first glance, you might think this is a quilt for a child. We think children would love it, but this quilt was actually commissioned by a Montessori school teacher. It was made for the top of a queen-size bed. If you'd like to make this quilt in a smaller size, see our suggestions on scaling in "The Size of Your Quilt" (page 56).

There are lots of ways you could vary the design of this quilt. One thing you could do is have the sun on the front of the quilt and the moon and stars on the back. Or you could make a sun that reverses to become the moon. As we were making this quilt, we came up with lots of sun-moon quilt designs. In fact, we could probably write a whole book on sun-moon quilts!

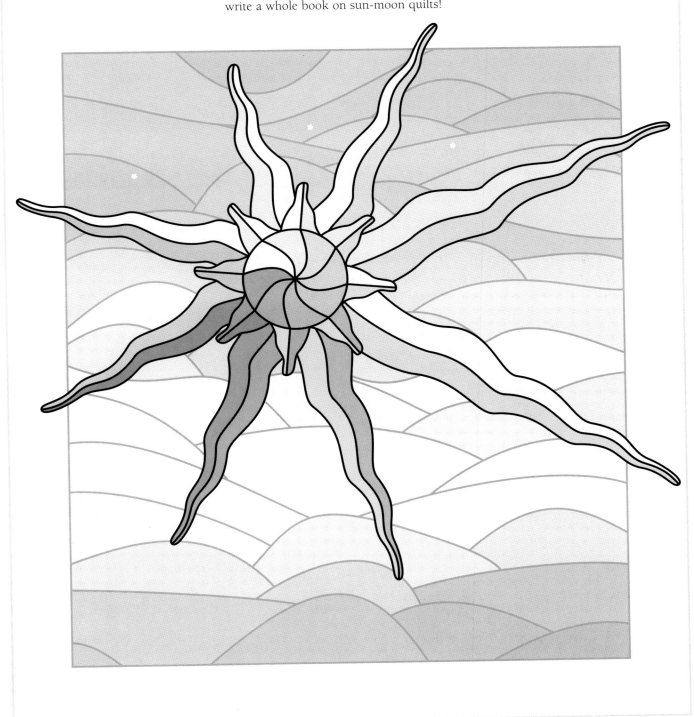

Main Diagram

WEE BAIRN

(from page 26)
Quilt Size: 40" x 40"

This baby quilt is made in the shape of a large flower. The center of the flower is surrounded by nine petals, each of which can be personalized as much or as little as you like. This is a manageable quilt to make because all of the petals are constructed separately and then attached to the center circle. There are also three "noisy toys" (a jingle bell, a squeaker and a rattle) that are hidden inside the three name petals. All of the fabrics for this quilt were chosen so that the finished product would be highly tactile in nature.

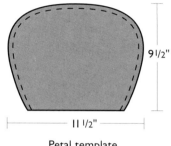

9 1/2"

11 1/2"

Petal template

6"

9"

15"

Leaf template

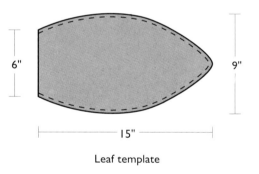

(Figure 1)

Materials & Cutting

Material	Amount	Use
Denim	10" x 12"	petal – name
Red Fleece	10" x 12"	petal – name
Wool Tartan	10" x 12"	petal – name
Red Berber	10" x 12"	petal – baby's hand
Gold Fun Fur	10" x 12"	petal – lion's paw
Orange Polar Fleece™	10" x 12"	petal – tiger's paw
Various Fabric Scraps		building petal fronts
Unbleached Cotton	3 of 10" x 12"	backing for piecing the landscapes
Green Polar Fleece™	25" x 25"	center of flower, cut into a circle
	9 of 10" x 12"	backings for all petals
Blue Polar Fleece™	25" x 25"	backing of flower, cut into a circle
Green & Blue Corduroy	18 of 9" x 15"	leaves
7-oz Batting	1 of 25" x 25"	batting for center, cut into a circle
	9 of 10" x 12"	batting for petals
	9 of 9" x 15"	batting for leaves

TOTAL Green Polar Fleece™ = 1.5 yd (45" width) / 1.4 m (110 cm width)
TOTAL Blue Polar Fleece™ = .75 yd (45" width) / .65 m (110 cm width)

All petal and leaf pieces are cut into the shapes shown in Figure 1.

Piecing

The nine petals are constructed first, with the top piecing described in three groups of three. The first group consists of landscapes, representing where the newborn's family is from. The second group consists of family names. The third group consists of "paw" prints, representing the baby's time of birth.

1

Landscape Petals These petals (prairie, ocean and mountains) are made using various techniques. The prairie hills and the ocean are constructed using the curved seam piecing technique (see "Curved Seam Piecing," page 59). The mountains are each made separately as lightly stuffed pieces, then they are all layered and appliquéd onto the blue sky backing. The cloud, hay bales and birds in the prairie scene, and the islands in the ocean scene, are also appliquéd.

2

Name Petals The three names were stitched using machine free-form stitching (see "Printing Text," page 58). In each case, a light piece of batting and a small piece of unbleached cotton were sandwiched together with the front piece of fabric. The unbleached cotton helps to give the piece some stability, especially when working with a stretchy fleece fabric. These layers were all pinned together, with the name written on top with chalk. Each name was stitched three times using a different color of thread each time.

3

Paw Petals   The three paw print petals are those of a lion, a tiger and of the
newborn. The animal prints were printed onto unbleached cotton with fabric paint
and a stamp made of foam pieces cut into the paw pad shapes. The handprint was
done using fabric paint (non-toxic, of course), which we painted onto the baby's
hand and then pressed onto unbleached cotton. For all three, the paint was set
using a hot iron. Each paw print was then used as the bottom piece of an inset
frame, which was set into the petal fabric (see "Inset Frames," page 61).
Alternatively, these could be appliquéd or printed directly onto your petal fabric.

4

Main Circle   The writing on the main circle was stitched in the same manner as
the name petals. Write your words on the top piece of fabric with chalk, then stitch
three times (using different colors of thread) through the sandwich of Polar
Fleece™, batting and unbleached cotton.

Finishing

5

Finish each of the petals by layering together the batting, the pieced top and the
Polar Fleece™ backing (right sides together). Stitch around the outside curved edge
using a ¹⁄₄" seam allowance (see "Inverse Batt Stitching," page 60). Trim and clip
seams, then turn right side out.

Inverse batt stitch the nine corduroy leaves in the same way.

6

Pin the petals and the leaves to the edge of the main circle, right sides together with
all pointing in (see Figure 2). Machine-baste the petals and leaves to the edge. Add
backing (right sides together) to sandwich and stitch around the circle, leaving one
petal open. Trim and clip seams, then turn flower right side out. Close the
remaining petal opening with hand-stitching on the top and bottom for strength.

Quilting

7

The final step is to stitch on the three central hearts. Cut out the hearts and baste
onto the front using a straight stitch. Appliqué the hearts though all layers using a
tight zigzag stitch.

Your Quilt

This quilt is very personal. Your quilt might look quite different, as it will reflect
your own family stories and heritage. Incorporate favorite family fabrics. How about
something from Mom's maternity clothes?

You could also add more petals to this quilt or, if you like, you could square off the
petals to make the whole thing look less like a flower. More colors could be added,
or you could change the back petal fabric so that it is different from the front. If
you have lots of things to add to the quilt, go ahead and run the stories and
memories on both sides.

*We appliquéd black strips onto
the orange Polar Fleece™ to
make tiger stripes.*

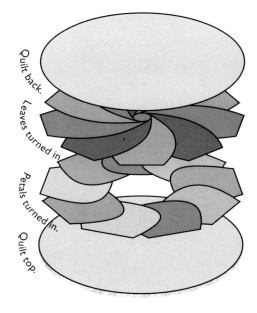

Quilt back.

Leaves turned in.

Petals turned in.

Quilt top.

(Figure 2)

*We slipped noisy toys into the name
petals (rattle, jingle, squeak). If you
do the same, then stuff these petals
a little more so that no toy edges
can be felt.*

CABIN FEVER

5 1/2"

A

2 1/4"

(Figure 1)

The game boards and appliquéd pieces incorporate a wide variety of fabric, including corduroy, cotton, flannel, velvet, rayon, denim and linen.

(from page 28)
Quilt Size: 56" x 72"
             80" x 72" (with pockets)

We chose the games for this quilt based on their relative ease of construction and, well, they were the ones we wanted to play! The blue side of the quilt features chess/checkers and a generic board game; the wine side features backgammon and cribbage. The side pockets were added so that the game pieces could be stored close by for those heated matches that last well into the middle of the night!

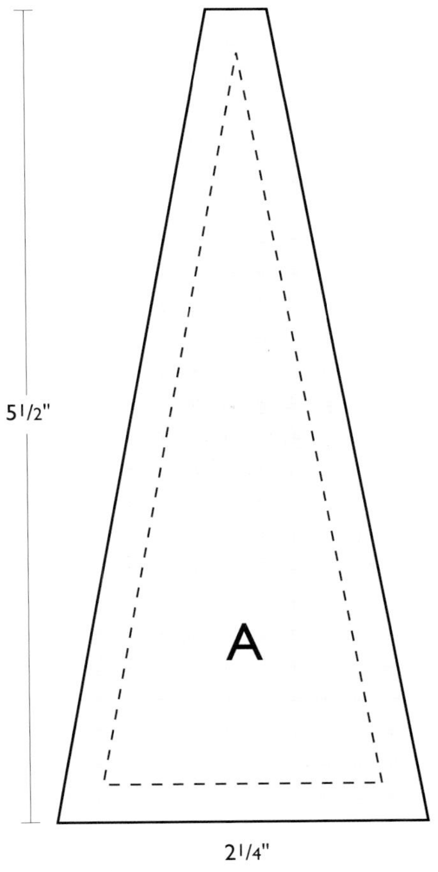

Materials & Cutting

Material	Amount	Use
Blue	32 of $2\frac{1}{2}$" x $2\frac{1}{2}$"	chess board
Green	32 of $2\frac{1}{2}$" x $2\frac{1}{2}$"	
Unbleached Cotton	4 of $2\frac{1}{2}$" x $18\frac{1}{2}$"	chess border
Various Fabrics	51 of $3\frac{1}{2}$" x $4\frac{3}{4}$"	board game
Unbleached Cotton	$1\frac{1}{4}$" x 280"	board game trim
	8 of 1" x $2\frac{1}{2}$"	instruction pillows
Patterned Wine	22 of Triangle A	backgammon board
Plain Wine	12 of Triangle A	
	2 of $2\frac{1}{2}$" x $9\frac{1}{2}$"	
Brown	12 of Triangle A	
	3 of $2\frac{1}{2}$" x $12\frac{1}{2}$"	backgammon border
	2 of $2\frac{1}{2}$" x $27\frac{1}{2}$"	
Unbleached Cotton	2 of $2\frac{1}{2}$" x $16\frac{1}{2}$"	
	2 of $2\frac{1}{2}$" x $31\frac{1}{2}$"	
Various Fabrics	24 of 4" x 7"	cribbage
Cheesecloth	24 of 4" x 7"	
Blue Cotton	$56\frac{1}{2}$" x $72\frac{1}{2}$"	foundation
Wine Cotton	$56\frac{1}{2}$" x $72\frac{1}{2}$"	
Unbleached Cotton	2 of 27" x 74"	side pockets
Various Fabrics		pocket squares, triangles and cribbage end square
3-oz Batting	2 of 56" x 72"	
16 Buttons		

TOTAL Blue Cotton = 2.25 yd (60" width) / 2 m (150 cm width)
TOTAL Wine Cotton = 2.25 yd (60" width) / 2 m (150 cm width)

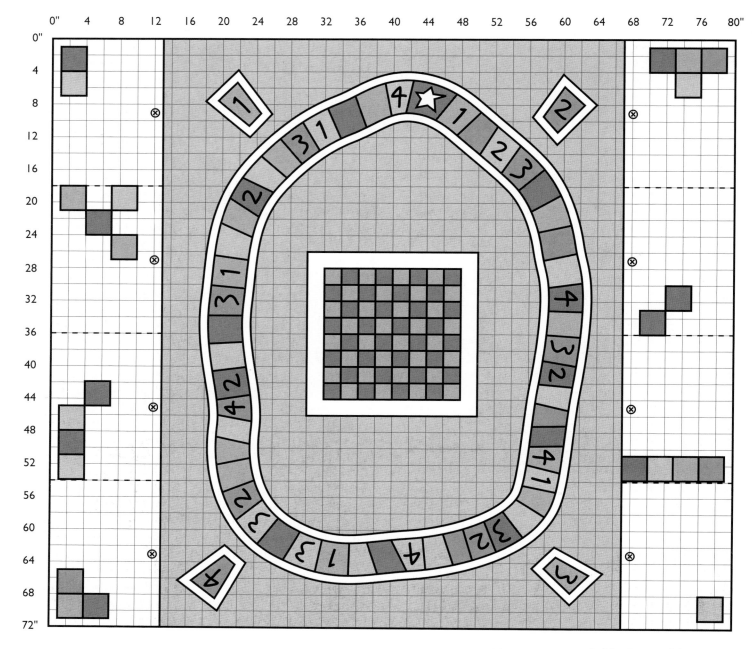

Main Diagrams - **Cabin Fever (blue side)**

Piecing

1

Chess/Checker Board The chess/checker board piecing can be completed by cutting and piecing all of the squares individually, or if you want to save a step, you can use a strip piecing technique. Cut the blue and green pieces into strips 2½" wide. Stitch a blue and green strip together, then cut them into the 2½" squares. Now stitch the pairs of squares together in rows, then stitch the rows together, matching intersecting seams. Attach a border of unbleached cotton on all sides. Press all seams, and press under ¼" on the unfinished border edge. Center the board on the blue foundation and topstitch close to the border edge. Topstitch again just inside the border on the game board.

When designing our game, we made sure that you couldn't lose a turn after moving back two spaces — that would just be too cruel!

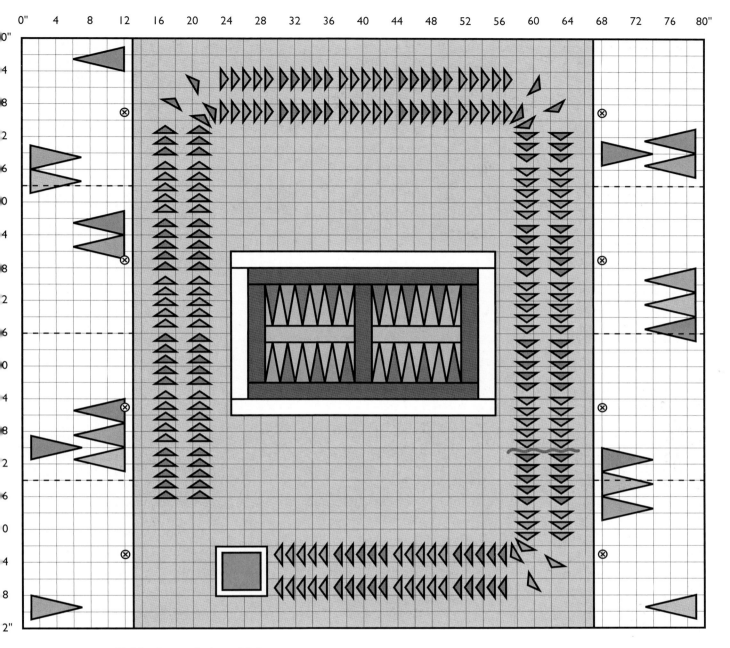

Main Diagrams - **Cabin Fever (wine side)**

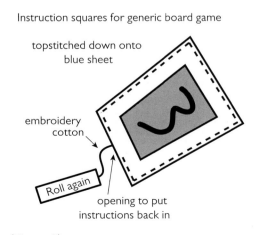

Instruction squares for generic board game

topstitched down onto
blue sheet

embroidery
cotton

Roll again

opening to put
instructions back in

(Figure 2)

2

Board Game on Blue Side   This is a generic game of our own invention. Our four corner pieces house the following instructions: 1. "Move Ahead 3 Spaces," 2. "Move Back 2 Spaces," 3. "Roll Again" and 4. "Lose a Turn." The instructions are written on little pillows tucked inside the corners.

To make the board, stitch the first square onto the blue foundation along the square's two side edges. Continue piecing the board by placing the next square right side down on the previous square and stitching the connecting seam through the foundation. Press the new piece out flat. Stitch all pieces down in this manner, with the final piece being topstitched down onto the first square. The unbleached cotton trim will finish off the side edges of your game board. Iron under ¼" along one edge of all your cotton strips – this will be the trim's finished outside edge. With right sides together and raw edges even, stitch the trim to the outside edge of the game squares using a ¼" seam allowance. We found it easier to piece the strips together as we went along and used bias strips at the curves. Where the trim meets itself, finish the join with hand-stitching, tucking one end into the other. Fold the trim out, press and topstitch the outside edge onto the blue sheeting. Repeat for the inside trim.

3

To make the instruction pillows, stitch two pieces of unbleached cotton together, leaving an opening at one end. Turn, press and stuff loosely with batting. Stitch opening closed. Use a fabric pen to write the instructions on the pillows. Now add an unbleached cotton border to all sides of the four corner pieces and press the raw edge under. The top edge should be folded under twice so it won't fray when the pillow is pulled out. Secure the instruction pillow to the border with embroidery cotton (see Figure 2). Topstitch the completed corner pieces to the foundation, leaving a 1½" opening at the top edge through which the little instruction pillow can be pulled when needed.

4

Backgammon Board   Stitch the triangles together first, then the middle wine rectangles and, finally, the brown and unbleached cotton borders. It is important to keep all seam allowances even so that the triangles will fit together precisely. Press all seams, and press under ¼" on the unfinished border edge. Topstitch onto the center of the large wine foundation, as you did with the chess/checker board (see Step 1).

5

Cribbage Board   Use the inset frame technique to complete the cribbage board (see "Inset Frames," page 61). First, determine the layout of your cribbage board around the outside of the wine sheet. Draw the triangles onto the cheesecloth strips. Place the cheesecloth strips on top of the sheet (right sides together) and stitch triangles as shown (see Figure 3). Cut the cheesecloth apart around each stitched triangle, then cut the triangle shape out through both layers and clip. Flip the cheesecloth through to the back and press. Behind each run of five pairs of triangles, place one of the fabric rectangles and topstitch around each triangle, as close to the edge as possible. Trim any excess overlap from the back. Stitch the corner pair of triangles along a diagonal line. There are 120 pairs of triangles, and the finishing square - the first one to 121 wins the game.

6

Construct your finishing square by stitching leftover strips of fabric together until a 4½" x 5½" square is made. Edge the square with an unbleached cotton border. Topstitch the finishing square into place. You can also stitch in your skunk line now – it goes between the 90th and 91st pairs of triangles.

7

Side Pockets   For the side pockets, fold each of the two long pieces of unbleached cotton in half lengthwise and press. Open the pockets back out. On one half of each long pocket, appliqué a random pattern of squares; on the other half, appliqué a random pattern of triangles (see Figure 4). Finish the top raw edge by folding it over twice and stitching. With right sides together, stitch the pockets together at each end. Turn right side out and press. Buttonholes were sewn on the top edge of each pocket at regular intervals. The buttonholes need to be in the same location on both sides of the pockets. Stitch the sides of the pockets together on the center line between each set of buttonholes to form smaller individual pockets (this will keep your game pieces better organized).

The cribbage board is quite involved. For us, it was easiest to cut an 8" strip off each outside edge of the foundation sheet. The cribbage triangles were stitched into the 8" strips and after the whole foundation was pieced back together.

1. mark triangles on cheesecloth

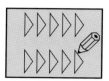

2. Place cheesecloth on wine foundation and stitch around triangles

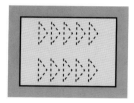

3. Cut out triangles and clip corners

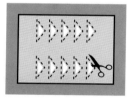

4. Cut cheesecloth (only) around triangles

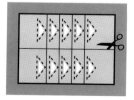

5. Push cheesecloth to back & press. Back with colored fabric and topstitch.

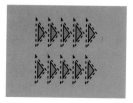

(Figure 3)

Quilting

8

Place a light sheet of batting behind each completed game sheet. On the blue side, quilt squares in random locations through the sheet and batting. On the wine side, quilt triangles. Quilt around the center game boards as well (use the outside stitching line that you topstitched previously as a guide).

Finishing

9

With right sides of the quilt together, stitch around the entire quilt, leaving a small section on the long edge open through which to turn the quilt. Trim seams and turn right side out. Finish opening with hand-stitching. Sew pairs of buttons back to back, matching their placement on each side of the quilt. Button on the pockets. Tack the pockets at the four corners right onto the quilt.

Your Quilt

For this project, the most obvious variation would be to quilt **your** favorite games. If your games are a little too hard to reproduce by quilting (e.g., a Scrabble™ board!), you might try using fabric paints instead.

We wanted to make our quilt reversible, with various games on either side. However, you can make things a little easier on yourself by only piecing games onto one side of the quilt.

Side Pockets (x 2)

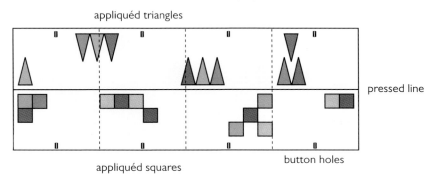

appliquéd triangles

pressed line

appliquéd squares

button holes

(Figure 4)

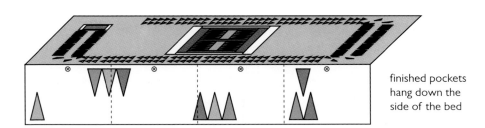

finished pockets hang down the side of the bed

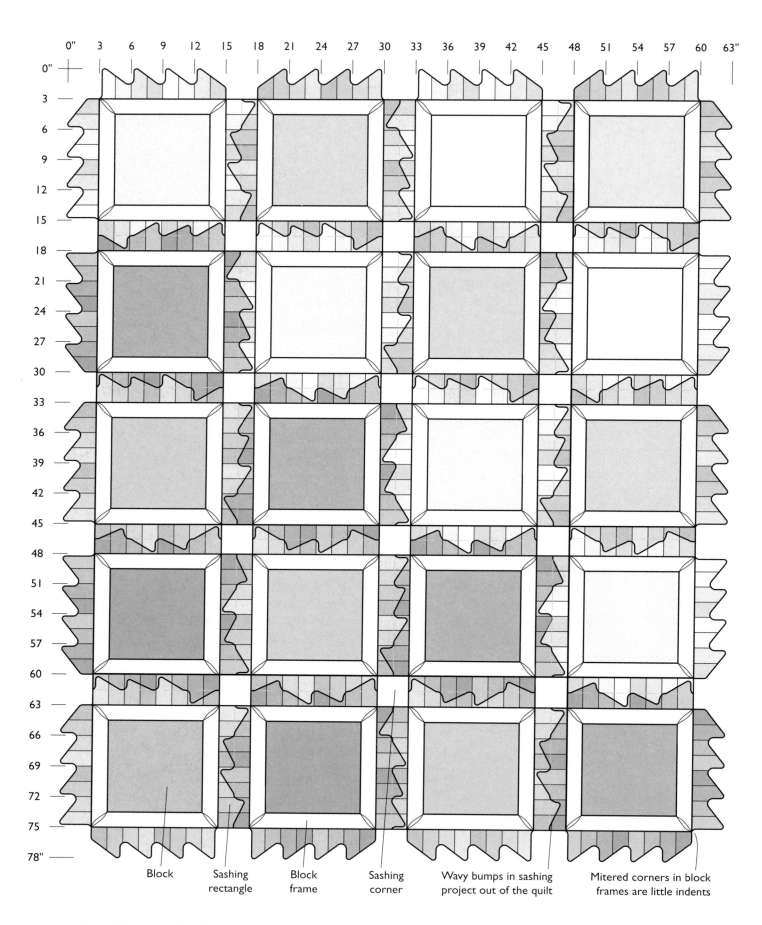

| | 0" | 3 | 6 | 9 | 12 | 15 | 18 | 21 | 24 | 27 | 30 | 33 | 36 | 39 | 42 | 45 | 48 | 51 | 54 | 57 | 60 | 63" |

Block

Sashing
rectangle

Block
frame

Sashing
corner

Wavy bumps in sashing
project out of the quilt

Mitered corners in block
frames are little indents

Main Diagram - **Tangible**

TANGIBLE

(from page 32)
Quilt Size: 63" × 78"

Fabric is so tactile, it surprises us that quilting projects don't focus more on the sensation of touch. This quilt uses a lot of tactile fabrics and is sewn so that the surface is not flat.

Materials & Cutting

Material	Amount	Use
Assorted Oranges	8 of 9½" x 9½"	large colored squares
Assorted Yellows	5 of 9½" x 9½"	large colored squares
Assorted Reds	5 of 9½" x 9½"	large colored squares
Assorted Oranges	160 of 2" x 6"	wavy sashing rectangles
Assorted Yellows	120 of 2" x 6"	wavy sashing rectangles
Assorted Reds	120 of 2" x 6"	wavy sashing rectangles
Cream Flannel	80 of 2" x 12½"	frames around large colored squares
	12 of 3½" x 3½"	sashing corners
	57½" x 72½"	backing
7-oz Batting	2 of 57½" x 72½"	
3-oz Batting	25" x 50"	batting for the wavy blocks

TOTAL Cream Flannel = 3 yd (60" width) / 2.75 m (150 cm width)

For assorted fabrics, we chose four velvets, three peach skins (a type of satin), two corduroys (one with a large wale and one with a fine wale) and one berber (sort of a faux lambskin). We also threw in a little Polar Fleece™, flannel and fun fur for good measure. Tactile soup! For colors, we chose vibrant oranges, yellows and reds. In laying out the colors we went from dark in the lower left corner to light in the upper right corner.

The peach skin material was really too slippery to work with, so we backed it with some interfacing. When working with the fun fur and its huge nap, we cut the material oversized and used larger than average seam allowances, which we trimmed after stitching.

Piecing

1

Blocks   Start with the cream flannel, which frames the large colored squares. The flannel pieces are 3" longer than the sides of each square. Set one square and one flannel piece right sides together along an edge so that the frame extends beyond the square 1½" on each end. Stitch these pieces using a ¼" seam allowance, starting and ending ¼" from the end. Use back-stitching to secure.

This quilt has some parts that stick out and some that stick in. Once you get the hang of making these indents and outdents, you'll see that it isn't too tough.

At one of the corners of the square, match the two flannel pieces right sides together. If you wanted a mitered corner here, you would sew a diagonal line. Instead, sew an "L" shape, as shown in Figure 1. This creates a bump that can either pop in or out of the quilting surface. Eventually these will be indents. Repeat this step for the remaining three corners. Frame all 20 colored squares the same way.

2

Sashing   Next, piece the colored wavy sashing rectangles, which join the framed blocks and stand up from the quilt surface. Rather than attempt to piece these one piece at a time, make two of the finished wavy blocks at once, as follows:

Using eight 2" x 6" pieces of fabric from one color group, piece them to make a 12½" x 6" rectangle, as shown in Figure 2. Repeat for the remaining 2" x 6" pieces. You should end up with 20 of the orange blocks and 15 each of the yellow and red blocks.

3

With one of the yellow and one of the orange 12½" x 6" rectangles (placed right sides together and with batting underneath), stitch the blocks together twice, using the wave shape. Cut between the two seams, clip the curves and turn right side out. You now have two finished orange-yellow wavy blocks that measure 12½" x 3½". Repeat these steps until you have produced 12 orange-yellow blocks, 12 orange-red blocks and 9 yellow-red blocks.

4

To make the wave shapes for the edge of the quilt, repeat Step 3 using the second wave pattern (see Figure 3). Make eight orange-yellow blocks, eight orange-red blocks and two yellow-red blocks. Set these border blocks aside.

5

Piecing the Top   Using the diagram and quilt photo as a guide, sew the framed blocks, sashing and sashing corners into rows, then stitch the rows together. Be careful not to catch the wavy bumps in your seams. Now you're ready for quilting.

For Tangible, we used lots of batting, which made quilting a little tougher than usual. Our objective in quilting was to recess the cream flannel (both block frames and sashing corners) and to elevate the rest of the quilt. With so much batting, the large colored squares pop up like little pillows, inviting hands to touch and tired heads to rest.

Stitch 4 frame pieces to colored squares. Stop ¼" from square's end, leaving frame ends free.

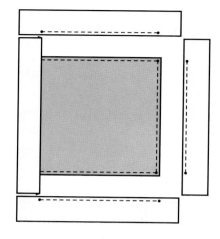

Fold the colored square along a diagonal and match the frame ends right sides together.

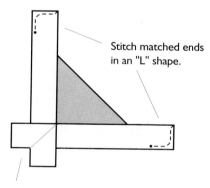

Stitch matched ends in an "L" shape.

Open up and refold on the other diagonal. Repeat for the remaining two corners.

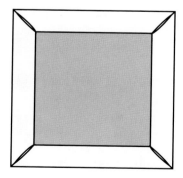

Open up and press flat. Corners look mitered but they're actually little pockets.

(Figure 1)

Stitch 8 of the 2" x 6" pieces
from the same color group
to make the rectangles first.

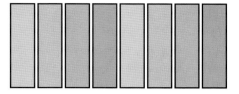

Make an inverse batt sandwich
with rectangles from two
different color groups.

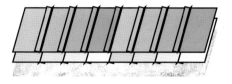

Stitch in a double wave pattern
and then cut between the seams.

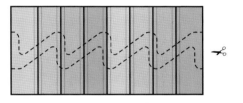

Clip curves and turn right sides out
to make two wave sashing rectangles.

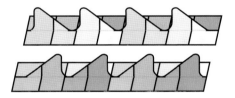

(Figure 2)

The wave pattern for the sashing
on the edge of the quilt is different.

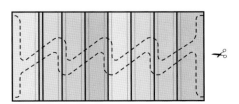

(Figure 3)

Quilting

6

Pin or baste the pieced front to two layers of batting (no back yet). Quilt around the wavy sashing rectangles along the seam lines. This is best accomplished by quilting horizontal and then vertical lines along the entire length (and width) of the quilt, rather than trying to quilt around one block at a time. Use a walking foot if possible.

7

Next quilt the lines in the block frames, offsetting them $3/8$" from the edge of the large colored squares. Notice that these lines don't actually meet. This is so you don't stitch over the indents at the corners of each square. Once again, it's easier to quilt these as a series of horizontal lines followed by a series of vertical lines. The final quilting will take place after the back is on.

Finishing

8

Pin the border wave pieces to the front of the quilt, matching the raw edges and lining them up with the blocks. The waves will all be facing in toward the center of the quilt. Now set the quilt back on top, right side down, and pin in place. Stitch around the edge of the quilt, leaving about 12" open on one edge. Turn the quilt right side out through this opening and finish the seam with top-stitching or by hand.

9

With the back in place, you can add the final quilting. Quilt around the small sashing corners $3/8$" from the edge. Add two fish, and you're done.

Your Quilt

Make this quilt uniquely your own by scaling it up or down, by changing the color scheme or by using a lot less batting so that you could add more quilting. If you don't like the idea of waves and indents, or find them too much of a challenge, you could simply create a flat quilt. The only thing we hope you don't change is the tactile choice of fabrics. You don't have to choose the same fabrics that we did, but for this quilt, we hope you don't choose cotton only.

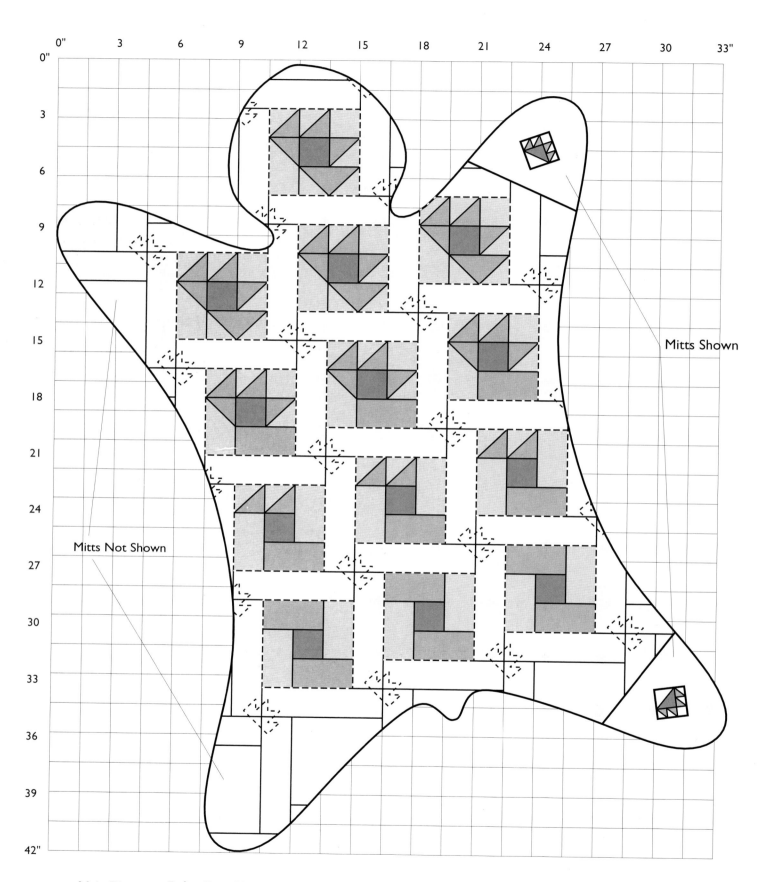

Main Diagram - **Baby Bear Hug**

BABY BEAR HUG

(from page 34)
Quilt Size: 27" x 39"
Block Size: 4½" x 4½"

This baby quilt has a pieced flannel front and a luxurious fun fur back, all in the shape of a wee bear. The flannel blocks slowly change from a bearpaw block at the top of the quilt down to a log cabin block at the tail end – from Mother Earth to the hearth, all warm and cuddly. The colors of the quilt signify the four elements – water (blue), fire (red), earth (brown) and air (cream). The blocks are primarily blue and red, with a little bit of red at the center of each one. Cream-colored flannel sashing outlines all of the blocks, and there are also four little mitts at the end of each leg for little hands and feet to tuck into. The mitts are reversible, so they can be flipped to the front or the back of the quilt.

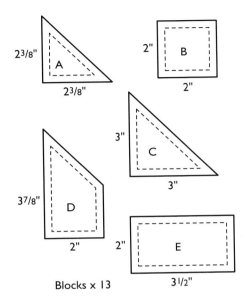

Blocks x 13

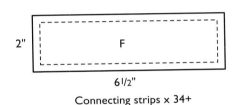

Connecting strips x 34+

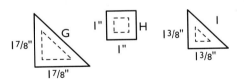

Tiny bear paw blocks inset in mitts x 4

Materials & Cutting

Material	Amount		Block	Pieces per Block
Cream Flannel	30" x 42"		Bearpaw (Row 1)	9 A, 2 B, 1 C, 1 D
Printed Flannels	18" x 42"		Row 2	7 A, 2 B, 1 D, 1 E
Fun Fur	30" x 42"		Row 3	4 A, 1 B, 3 D
3-oz Batting	30" x 42"		Log Cabin (Row 4)	1 B, 4 E
7-oz Batting	30" x 10"		Tiny Bearpaw	2 G, 2 H, 8 I

This quilt is an irregular shape, so it makes for some odd-sized pieces around the edge of the quilt. Rather than cut these to fit, we pieced in extra flannel to fill out the full quilt, then cut the bear shape in the final stage. Similarly, the fun fur backing and the mitts were cut oversized and trimmed afterwards (see Figure 1). Each mitt has a cream front with an inset tiny bearpaw block and a colored back.

In the cutting and piecing diagrams we show pieces for the bearpaw block and the log cabin block, as well as for the two blocks used for the transition from bearpaw to log cabin. If you look closely at our blocks, you will see some slight variations from traditional blocks. These variations were designed to make the transition from bearpaw to log cabin work and to complement the rotation of the blocks and the pattern of the sashing.

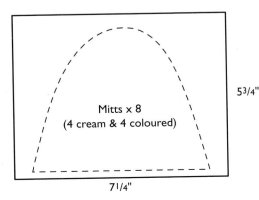

Mitts x 8
(4 cream & 4 coloured)

(Figure 1)

Piecing

1

Piece together the 13 blocks according to the piecing diagrams, using a ¼" seam allowance (see Figure 2). Press all completed blocks. Attach the sashing to the blocks, building one row at a time (see Figure 3). Continue the pattern of blocks and sashing to fill out the bear shape. We used cream flannel pieces for the background and sashing.

2

To assemble the bearpaw mitts, piece the tiny bearpaw blocks and inset these into the cream front of the mitt using the inset frame technique (see "Inset Frames," page 61). With the colored back of the mitt, stitch the mitts right sides together along the bottom seam only. Fold the mitts right side out, press and set aside until the quilting is complete (Step 5).

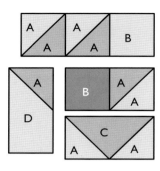

Bear paw block assembly

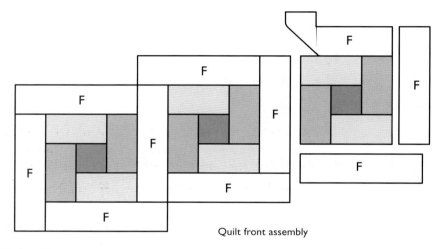

Quilt front assembly

(Figure 3)

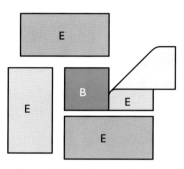

Log cabin block assembly

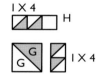

Tiny bear paw
inset block assembly

(Figure 2)

Quilting

3

For quilting, we used a 3-oz sheet of batting. We also added an extra piece of 7-oz batting in behind each of the center blocks. This raises the blocks up and gives the quilt a softer appearance.

The quilting consists of stitching around each block close to the seam, as well as stitching a little bearpaw outline at each sashing intersection (see Figure 4). Use a template to trace the bearpaw outline onto the pieced front to guide the quilting. We did all the quilting by machine.

We did the quilting before the backing went on because we didn't want to quilt through the oh-so-rich fun fur.

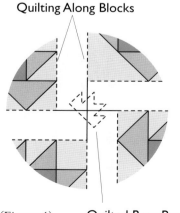

Quilting Along Blocks

(Figure 4)   Quilted Bear Paw

Finishing

4

Now it's time to make the quilted front closer to the final shape of the bearskin rug. On the front of the quilt, mark the outline of the bear with a $1/2$" seam allowance. (This seam allowance needs to be larger than usual due to the heavy backing fabric and tricky shape.) To transfer this shape onto the front of the quilt, you can either cut a bear-shape pattern out of paper or measure from the diagram. Cut the front of the quilt (including the batting) to this shape.

5

Next, baste the mitts in place onto the front of the quilt. We basted the mitts so that the colored plain side faces the right side of the flannel front. Now place the front of the quilt right side down onto the uncut fun fur piece. This would be a good time to use a walking foot or feed foot on the sewing machine if you have one. Stitch the outside seam all around, leaving a gap (around 6") near the tail to pull the quilt through. Trim seams, clip curves. Pull the quilt through and finish the opening by hand-stitching. Remove any exposed basting. Pull out any fur caught in the seam – a knitting needle may be helpful for this step. Add two fish, and you're done.

Your Quilt

Rich fun fur is beautiful, but it's tough to work with. You could try a berber or Polar Fleece™ instead. But if you're willing to take the fun fur plunge (and it's worth it), the possibilities are virtually endless. How about a white fun fur backing for a cold climate polar bear? Or how about other animal shapes? Tiger? Zebra? Orangutan? Pig? Poodle?

When we finished our quilt, we were disappointed that it was baby-size. I mean, it's so luxurious, we wanted to stretch out on it ourselves. Can you imagine a full-size grizzly bear quilt for two to curl up on in front of the fireplace? Mmmmmm.

It's important to pin or baste everything down tightly because the fun fur has a huge nap, which shifts everything around. This nap problem is why we didn't cut the backing ahead of time.

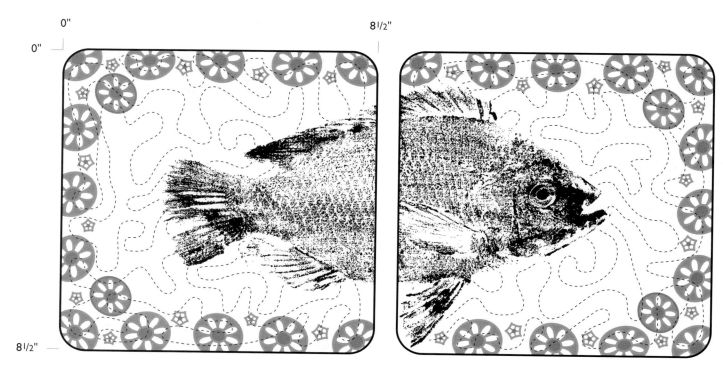

0"   8½"

0"

8½"

Main Diagram

FISH ON FRIDAYS

(from page 38)
Block Size: 8½" x 8½"

This is the easiest project in the book, simply because of its size. The centerpiece of these quilted trivets/pot holders uses **Gyotaku**, the ancient Japanese art of fish printing. The result is amazingly lifelike (**fishlike?**). The border is decorated with prints of exotic vegetables.

Materials & Cutting

Material	Amount	Use
Unbleached Cotton	3 of 9" x 18"	printing the fish
Heat Shield Padding	1 of 9" x 18"	acts as batting and
		protects your hands
Cotton Broadcloth	2 of 9" x 9"	backing
Polar Fleece™	2 of 9" x 9"	holes for hands
Fish	1	
Vegetables		
Fabric Paints		

When we made these trivets/pot holders, we cut the material oversized from the precise dimensions listed above and trimmed after stitching. This makes centering the fish less difficult and also eases the stitching through the six layers when you are finishing the piece. Make sure to prewash and press the material well for the printing.

For the fish, we chose a tilapia. When you choose your fish, here are a few things to keep in mind: You need a whole fresh fish, not one that's been gutted; you need a fish that fits the size of your pot holders (our tilapia was 11" long and 5" wide); a fish with prominent scales works better than a smooth fish; and a flat fish works better than a round fish. We found our fish down at the local fish market for under two dollars.

For the vegetables, we chose okra and lotus root. Potato prints would have also worked well, or cut cabbage, mushrooms ... whatever your favorite vegetables might be.

Piecing

1

For each of the pot holders, place the cotton backing and Polar Fleece™ right sides together and stitch a 3½" diameter hole using the inset frame technique (see "Inset Frames," page 61). Cut out the circle, turn right side out and set aside.

Printing

2

That's it for piecing, but before you quilt, you'll need to print the fish. If you discover that this is something that you really enjoy, there are whole books on **Gyotaku**. A crash course is described here. Remember, you'll need prewashed, pressed fabric.

- Work with the fish as soon as you can, because the fresher the better. Clear eyes are a good indication of a fresh fish. You won't have to worry about any bad smell, as long as you get rid of the fish slime first (see next step).
- Rinse the slime off the fish.
- Rub it lightly with some salt and rinse it again (this gets the last of the slime off).
- Dry the fish thoroughly.
- Stuff some newspaper or paper towel into the openings – gills, mouth and, yep, the bum.
- Lay the fish onto some newspaper.
- Brush the fabric paint on the side of the fish that's facing up. Don't forget to paint the fins. You'll want to experiment a bit with how much paint to use. Use brush strokes that go from head to tail or from tail to head rather than across the fish. Don't put paint on the eye. Transfer the fish to clean newspaper.
- While the paint is still wet, lay the fabric face down on the fish. Work from the center of the fish toward the edges and, with your hands, press the material firmly to the fish. You might even want to hold the fins out to get a more dramatic effect.
- Remove the fabric. Touch up any areas with a brush. Paint the eye.

We printed the fish on two of the three pieces of unbleached cotton, one print from each side of the fish.

If you don't stuff the fish openings, then when you press the cloth onto the fish it will ooze stuff out of these locations.

3

Next print the border using the cut vegetables that you have chosen. Experiment with the cut vegetables by brushing paint on them or dipping them until you find the right effect. Let the paint dry on the fabric and then set it with a hot, dry iron. Don't wash the fabric for at least three days after the printing to allow the paint to set.

Quilting

4

Choose which of the two fish prints you like best. Make a sandwich with the best print right side up on top, unprinted piece of unbleached cotton next, heat shield padding next and second best fish print right side down on the bottom (see Figure 1). Quilt this sandwich from outside the fish all the way to the border using squiggly lines. This quilting is accomplished by setting the stitch length to zero, reducing the pressure of the foot on your machine, holding the fabric tightly and moving it in a free-form manner.

We think this "meander" quilting pattern looks like coral.

Finishing

5

You should now have one quilted top (that will become two in a minute) and two bottoms with holes. Pin the two bottoms to the top, right sides together. Stitch the two $8\frac{1}{2}$" squares. Cut the top piece in half between the stitching lines, trim the seams and turn the pot holders right side out. You've already added two fish, so you're done!

Best print face up

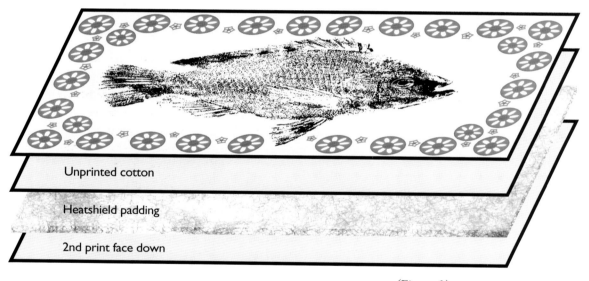

Unprinted cotton

Heatshield padding

2nd print face down

(Figure 1)

Your Quilt

Gyotaku is pretty simple, and we were able to get lovely prints without much effort. If you like Gyotaku, then you might want to incorporate it into placemats or even a full-size quilt. Be creative with the vegetable printing. After we were done, someone suggested printing with a cabbage cut in a cross-section. We thought it would look a lot like flowing water.

If you don't like Gyotaku, then might we suggest children's art as an alternative? One of our ideas was to take the kids' art that often adorns fridges and turn it into functional, pot holder art using photo-transfer. Better yet, have your children (or grandchildren) use fabric paints to create a picture for you straight onto canvas.

CLASSIC THEATER

(from page 40)
Quilt Size: 56" x 63"
Stage Size: 15" x 12"

This quilt would work equally well as a permanently hung finger puppet theater or as a quilt on a bed. When on a bed, your child could be both the puppeteer and the audience at the same time! We used a lot of machine washable velvet to give it a medieval theater feel. For this quilt, we refer to the side with the draped velvet as the front and the side with the four panels and the scroll work as the back.

Materials & Cutting

Material	Amount	Use
Purple Velvet	59" x 59"	draped front
	2 of 11" x 42"	pennants
	5½" x 40½"	hanging sleeve border
	2 of 15" x 28"	theater curtain
	4 of 3" x 15"	stage frame
	4 of 2" x 15"	backing of banners
	20½" x 25½"	back quarter panel
Green Velvet	2 of 11" x 42"	pennants
	5½" x 40½"	hanging sleeve border
	4 of 2" x 15"	front of banners
	20½" x 25½"	back quarter panel
Wine Velvet	10½" x 40½"	hanging sleeve border
	4 of 3" x 15"	stage frame
	2 of 20½" x 25½"	back quarter panel
Lining	3 of 11" x 42"	opening pennants
7-oz Batting	12" x 42"	batting for hanging loops
	12" x 26"	batting for lower pennants
	42" x 52"	quilt body and curtains
Purple Cord	42"	to hang the curtain on
Purple Separating Zippers	5 of 9"	opening pennants
Green Separating Zippers	5 of 9"	opening pennants
Snaps	18	for banners and curtains

The velvet material that we purchased for this quilt came in a 59" width. From the amounts specified, you should be able to cut all the pieces and still have scraps left over to use for the scroll work piecing on the back and other little details.

TOTAL Purple Velvet = 3.3 yd (60" width) / 3 m (150 cm width)
TOTAL Green Velvet = 1.2 yd (60" width) / 1.1 m (150 cm width)
TOTAL Wine Velvet = 1 yd (60" width) / .9 m (150 cm width)

Piecing

1

Piecing the Bottom Pennants The four pennants along the bottom of the quilt are straightforward triangles stuffed with batting. Make each pennant with one side green and the other side purple. Inverse batt stitch one pennant together (see "Inverse Batt Stitching," page 60), leaving open the side that attaches to the quilt. Turn the pennant right side out and finger press flat. Repeat for the other three pennants.

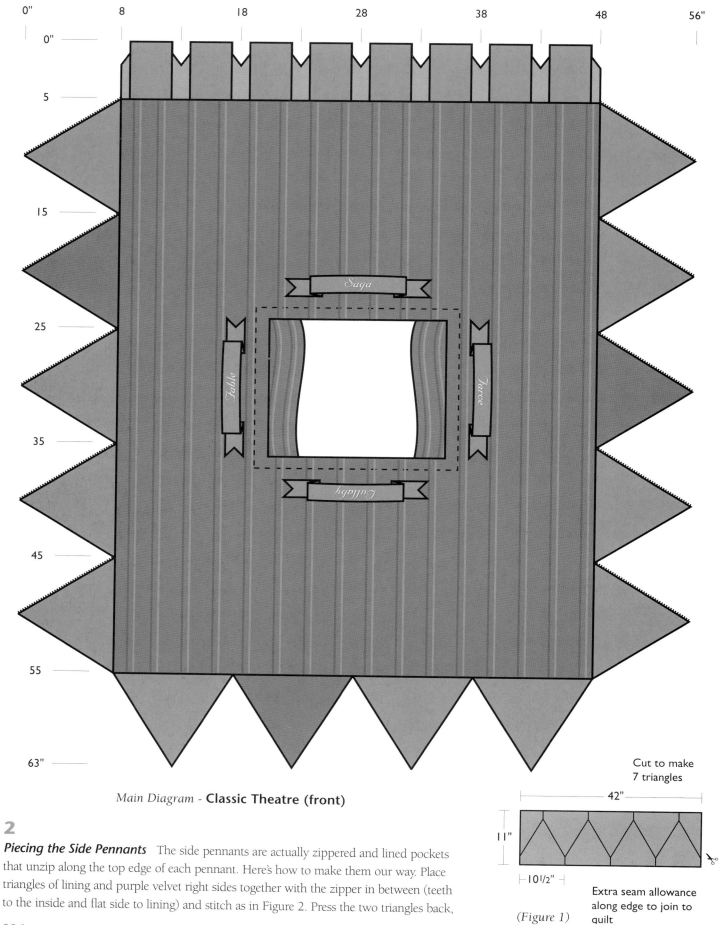

*Main Diagram - **Classic Theatre (front)***

Cut to make
7 triangles

42"

11"

10½"

(Figure 1)

Extra seam allowance
along edge to join to
quilt

2

Piecing the Side Pennants The side pennants are actually zippered and lined pockets that unzip along the top edge of each pennant. Here's how to make them our way. Place triangles of lining and purple velvet right sides together with the zipper in between (teeth to the inside and flat side to lining) and stitch as in Figure 2. Press the two triangles back,

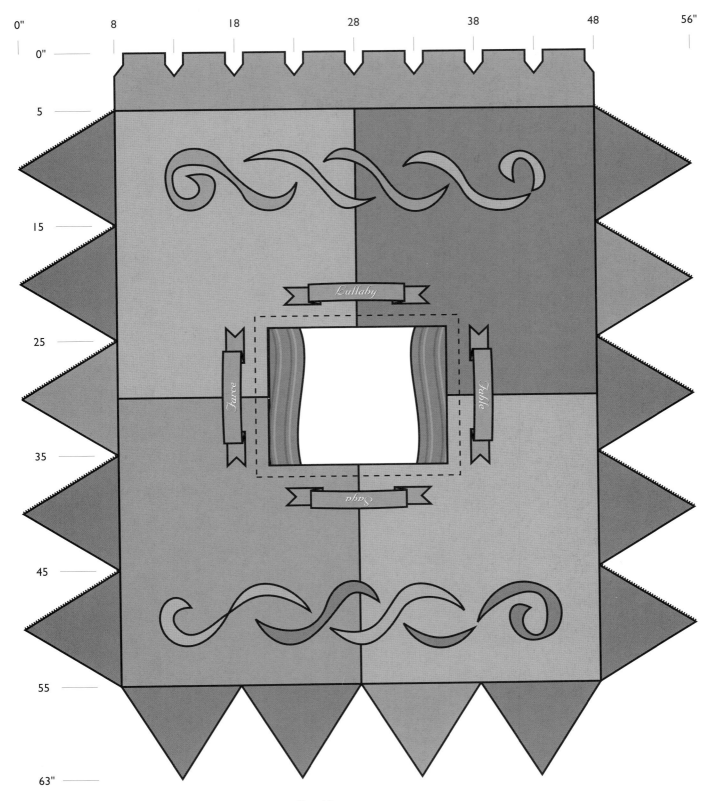

Main Diagram - **Classic Theatre (back)**

exposing the zipper. Repeat with a triangle of green velvet, lining and the other side of the zipper. Make sure you have the correct ends of the zippers placed so they will zip.

Match the raw edges of the lining together and stitch the bottom edge of the pennant. Leave open the edge that attaches to the quilt. Match the raw edges of the green and purple velvet triangles and stitch in the same way. Turn the velvet triangle right side out.

3

Piecing the Hanging Sleeve Border   Piece together the purple and green velvet sleeve border pieces along one long edge. This is the outside of the sleeve and the wine velvet piece is the inside of the sleeve. Mark the pattern shown in Figure 3 onto the wine piece. Inverse batt stitch the layers, trim the seams and clip. Turn right side out. Fold the sleeve in half, matching and pinning the unfinished edges. The wine side should be facing in and the purple/green side should be facing out.

4

Piecing the Front of the Quilt   The front of the quilt is very simple, deriving most of its beauty from the gathered draping of the purple velvet. Baste two rows ¼" apart across the top and bottom of the front of the quilt. Also, baste a double row 2" above and 2" below the location of the stage (for a length of 22½"). Pull the basting until the top and bottom are 40½" wide and the rows above and below the stage are 15" wide.

5

Piece the frame for the stage using the four 3" x 15" wine-colored pieces, as shown in Figure 4. Make an inset frame in the center of the gathered purple velvet front (see "Inset Frames," page 61). In this case, the difference in the inset frame is that a narrow facing is being used for the frame instead of a large rectangle. Cut out the hole, trim the edges, clip the seam allowances and push the frame to the inside. This inset frame will frame the hole for the stage.

6

Piecing the Back of the Quilt   Piece the back of the theater using the four quarter panels. Pin the pieced back onto the large sheet of batting. Piece together the four purple stage frame pieces, as in Step 5. Use the stage frame to make an inset frame, this time stitching and cutting through the batting as well. Cut out the hole, trim the edges, clip the seams and turn the frame to the inside. Reserve the batting you've just cut out for the theater curtain and the velvet for the scroll work piecing.

7

Piecing the Theater Curtains   Take one of the purple pieces for the theater curtain. Fold the piece in half crosswise, right sides together, and place it overtop a light piece of batting. The piece will now measure 15" x 14". Inverse batt stitch the top and bottom (see Figure 5). Turn right side out. Repeat for the other curtain. Thread the two curtain cords.

8

Piecing the Banners   We first had the words **Fable**, **Farce**, **Saga** and **Lullaby** commercially embroidered in gold thread onto the green velvet and then cut them out as pieces for the banners. You might have a machine that can embroider words or you can hand-embroider them. Take an embroidered green piece and purple back piece and inverse batt stitch the banner together (see Figure 6). Clip the corners, cut a slit (as shown) and turn the banner right side out. Hand-stitch the post halves of the snaps onto the banner where marked. Repeat for the other three banners.

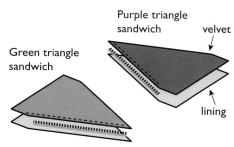

Stitch the zippers in the two halfs, then open and stitch the halves together.

(Figure 2)

You'll want to make sure that you sew half of the pennants with purple on the right side and green on the left side and half of the pennants the other way around.

Mark these picket shapes onto the back of the wine colored piece.

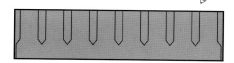

Inverse batt stitch the sleeve. Cut out the pickets, clip corners and turn right sides out.

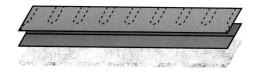

(Figure 3)

Depending on the thickness of your cord, you may need to make tiny holes in the folded edges of the curtains to feed the cord. We used an upholstery needle and fed the cord right through the seam at the corners. The tight fit creates friction, which helps the curtain stay put when it's open.

Piece frame together

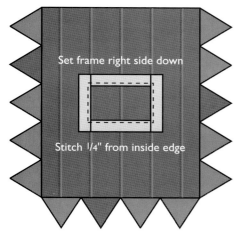

Set frame right side down

Stitch 1/4" from inside edge

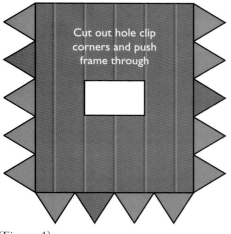

Cut out hole clip corners and push frame through

(Figure 4)

Curtain cord is threaded through on top...

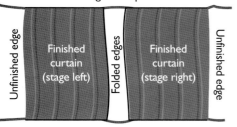

| Unfinished edge | Finished curtain (stage left) | Folded edges | Finished curtain (stage right) | Unfinished edge |

...and on the bottom

(Figure 5)

Quilting

9

We added the scroll work piecing to the back of the quilt between the stage and the top and bottom edges of the quilt. Use chalk to draw the scroll work onto some velvet scraps. Pin the scraps right side up onto the back of the quilt and stitch along the chalk lines through all layers (scraps, back and batting). Trim the scraps as tightly as possible to the seams. Finish these edges using a tight zigzag stitch in gold thread. The quilt batting is also held in place around the stage opening and along the outside seam edges, so no other top quilting was done.

Finishing

10

You're now ready to put the front and back together. Lay the back of the quilt down right side up. Place the pennants onto the back so that they are pointing toward the center of the quilt, zippers up. Pin these in place. Pin the sleeve border to the top of the quilt in the same manner. Next lay the front of the quilt right side down. Match edges and pin it all together. Stitch around the entire edge of the quilt, making sure to catch all layers. Turn the quilt right side out through the stage hole.

11

Pin the curtains in place in the stage opening. Baste, then stitch around the stage opening, making sure to catch the curtains and the curtain cord on the left and right sides of the opening. Be sure also that the curtains and cord are left free at the top and bottom of the opening. After you are finished sewing, open and close the curtain to ensure that everything works as it should. Secure the center of the curtain cord at the top and bottom of the opening. Hand sew on two snaps to close the curtain. Hand sew the bottoms of snaps onto the quilt front and back for the banners.

Your Quilt

This quilt used a lot of velvet, so it was more costly to create than the quilts we've made with salvaged fabrics. For variety and/or to save on costs, you could piece the front or back of your quilt from salvaged materials.

You might also like to do more quilting and switch the front to the back. Another interesting idea would be to quilt different backdrops. These could be pieced or painted and then buttoned or snapped on behind the stage opening. It would be a fun project to work on with children. Or maybe the natural draping of the velvet caught your eye as it did ours. Perhaps this shouldn't be a children's puppet theater after all, but rather a richly draped velvet quilt for your bed. Mmmmmm.

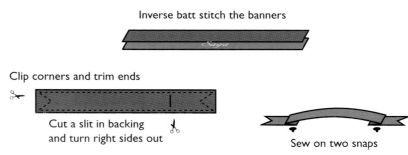

Inverse batt stitch the banners

Clip corners and trim ends

Cut a slit in backing and turn right sides out

Sew on two snaps

(Figure 6)

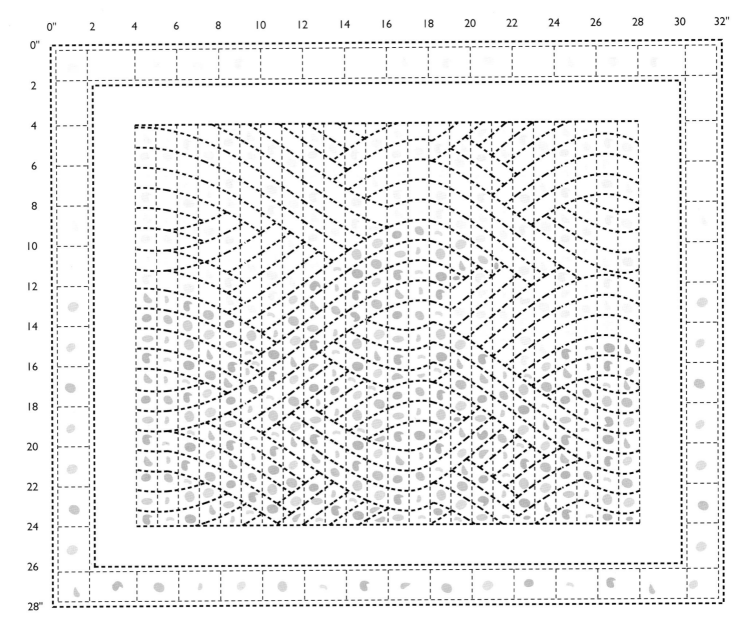

Main Diagram

TSUNAMI

(from page 44)
Mosaic Size: 28" x 33"

This quilted shower curtain is by far our most novel "quilt" idea. We took sea glass (or "beach" glass) and quilted it onto a clear plastic shower curtain using a backing of netting. The netting faces into the tub, and when the shower is on, the sea glass gets wet and glistens. The piece is simple, functional and very cool.

Materials & Cutting

Material	Amount	Use
Nylon Netting	35" x 40"	for holding the mosaic in place
Clear Plastic Shower Curtain		
Sea Glass, Sea Shells, etc.	as needed	for the mosaic

We're big fans of sea glass. We always look for it when we go to the beach. Sea glass can be found on most beaches, but there are definitely some beaches that are more bountiful than others. (Incidentally, blue sea glass is much less common than clear or green glass.)

We bought a shower curtain that was reinforced with grommets because the mosaic definitely adds extra weight to the piece. Try to find a strong yet unobtrusive netting. Most nylon netting is inherently weak and rips easily, but there are some nettings that have a tighter weave and are tougher. The netting is oversized to allow it to have a little bunching, which will provide room for the sea glass.

Laying Out the Mosaic

1

There is no piecing in this project, but there is the mosaic of a wavy sea silhouetted against a light sky. Draw out the mosaic onto a large piece of paper. Transfer the design onto the clear plastic shower curtain using a water soluble marker. Now set the sea glass mosaic out onto the piece of paper (i.e., not on the shower curtain yet).

Quilting

2

In our mosaic, the vertical columns were first quilted by machine and the horizontal lines of the waves and sky were later quilted by hand. Tape one edge of the netting onto the shower curtain. Stitch the first vertical line in the mosaic. For each of the subsequent lines, gather the netting in $\frac{1}{8}$" to $\frac{1}{4}$" (as shown in Figure 1) and stitch 1" apart. Stitch across the bottom of the mosaic, closing off one end of the channels.

3

A few pieces at a time, transfer the sea glass from the paper mosaic to the shower curtain mosaic. Drop them into the channel and push them into place (we used a knitting needle for this). Hand-quilt the horizontal lines to hold the sea glass in place. We used a heavy weight thread and chose navy blue for the sea and light blue for the sky. We used as small a needle as possible (and a thimble) to help in punching through the plastic of the shower curtain. When stitching in plastic you are actually making holes in the material, so the smaller the better. We used eight stitches per inch, and we were careful with tying knots and trimming tails, because there's nowhere to hide them.

Finishing

4

Once the mosaic was quilted in, we added a border of beach pebbles and sea shells. Again, machine-stitch a channel and insert the beach pebbles and sea shells. On the vertical sides of the border, we machine-stitched some short horizontal lines, making a ladder effect to separate the pebbles and shells. Finish with one final machine-stitch around the entire border, then simply trim the netting close to this stitch.

Stitch netting in vertical lines spaced 1" apart.

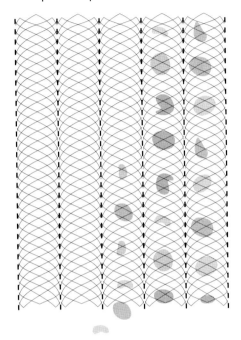

Don't stitch the netting flat. Leave room to slide the sea glass or sea shells in after.

(Figure 1)

Your Quilt

Before you quilt this shower curtain, we should point out that our mosaic weighed 2 lbs. You should first consider whether or not the curtain you are going to quilt on to, and the rod it will hang on, can handle the extra weight.

The hardest part of this project is finding the sea glass. However, the mosaic doesn't have to be made entirely of sea glass. You could use whatever sea glass you find and then fill in the rest with little shells or pieces of shells. Another possibility would be to use tiny pieces of driftwood. Not only are these things easier to find, but they will not make the shower curtain quite so heavy. You could also design a mosaic that uses fewer pieces of sea glass. Even something as straightforward as a coarse rectangular grid would be neat and easier to accomplish.

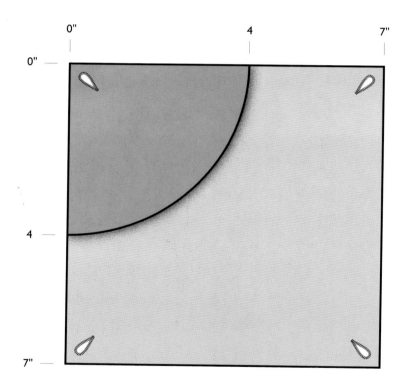

BUDDING POET

(from page 46)
Quilt Size: 42" x 56"
Block Size: 7" x 7"

This quilt is made up of 48 finished blocks that button together. It's an easy quilt to make, and you can add as many (or as few) blocks as you like. The words we used were chosen from a list made by our friends at a dinner party (see how sociable all this quilting can be?). Sorry Ellen, but we decided not to use your choice of **guppy** in the end.

Materials & Cutting (for 48 blocks)

Material	Amount	Use
Various Fabrics (purple)	24 of 7½" squares	Drunkard's Path block
	24 of 8½" semicircles	
Various Fabrics (green)	24 of 7½" squares	Drunkard's Path block
	24 of 8½" semicircles	
100% Cotton (green)	48 of 7½" squares	word block
7-oz Batting	48 of 7½" squares	
Buttons	100+	buttoning blocks

TOTAL Green Cotton = 2.2 yd (45" width) / 2 m (110 cm width)

Our green and purple fabrics for the Drunkard's Path blocks include cotton, brushed cotton, silk, wool, Polar Fleece™, corduroy and cotton/polyester blends. The number of buttons you need will depend on how the quilt is put together. make sure they are all the same size though.

Piecing

1

To assemble the Drunkard's Path blocks, begin by folding each semicircle in half, right sides together, and stitching along the curved edge using a ¼" seam allowance. Turn right side out and press. Pin each ¼ circle to the large colored squares in any corner, matching the edges.

Printing

2

Print each word onto the center of the plain cotton square (see "Printing Text," page 58, for options). The printing technique that we chose was to transfer photocopied words onto the fabric using acetone. It worked well for us, but acetone is not the nicest substance to work with (in terms of noxious fumes and corrosive action), so you may well want to make an alternate choice.

Quilting

3

The only quilting done in this project is on the word blocks. Layer the fabric (right side up) on a piece of batting and stitch a ¼ circle shape in one corner of the square. The size of the ¼ circle should be the same as that of the circle on the Drunkard's Path block. This will keep the Drunkard's Path theme running through both sides of the quilt.

We designed a variation of the Drunkard's Path, which allowed us to avoid hand-stitching and to finish the blocks cleanly. In the end, the 1/4 circles form little pockets, leaving the finished curved edge free.

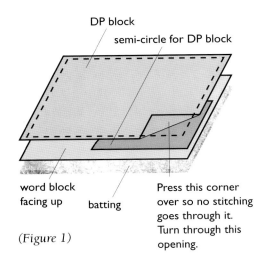

DP block
semi-circle for DP block
word block facing up
batting
Press this corner over so no stitching goes through it. Turn through this opening.

(Figure 1)

Finishing

4

Place the word block and the Drunkard's Path block right sides together. Align the sides so that the two ¼ circles are in the same corner. Stitch around each block. As you stitch around the corner that has the ¼ circle, fold a corner of the topmost fabric out of the way (see Figure 1). This will give you a hole through which to turn the entire block. Trim all corners and seam allowances, turn the block right side out and press. The opening is finished with a buttonhole (Step 5).

5

Stitching in the buttonholes is a big task because they are required at the four corners of 48 blocks! Stitch the buttonholes diagonally into the block (for strength) and as close to the edge as possible (so there is less block overlap).

6

We bought more than 100 "orphan" buttons (buttons that have lost their brothers and sisters) in colors reflected in the quilt blocks. The buttons are all the same size and are tied back to back in pairs. Use embroidery cotton or heavy thread, and leave a 1" gap between the buttons, as you need space to button four blocks together. We also wrapped the 1" gap with more thread for more strength.

Now compose a poem by buttoning your blocks together in any way you choose. It's that simple!

Your Quilt

The beauty of this quilt is that, if you like, you can keep expanding it . We completed 48 blocks, but you may choose to do many more (or many less!). The size of the blocks can also be varied quite easily. And because the arrangement of the blocks allows much flexibility, this quilt could be used as either a bed covering or a wall hanging.

A lot of flexibility also exists in designing the back of the blocks. We chose a Drunkard's Path, but any quilt block pattern can be used, or you could design your own. Another idea for the back of the blocks is a reproduction of your favorite painting. Abstract paintings might work best, but choose carefully – a Jackson Pollock would likely be pretty difficult to piece!

If the idea of making multiple blocks on your own doesn't entirely appeal to you, you could throw a quilt party in which everyone designs and completes one block (there's that social aspect again). The end product of this co-operative effort would work well as a going away gift or as a wedding present.

Remember that additional blocks can always be made at a later date. How about a baby quilt in which a new block is added at each birthday? Or a family history quilt in which each block represents one member of the family or a significant family occasion? The back of each of these blocks could be made of "memory" fabrics from favorite clothes donated by each family member.

Sewing the button holes severely tested our patience, so we suggest that you only stitch buttonholes into a few blocks per sitting, or beg/borrow a buttonhole machine to complete this step (or better yet, have a buttonhole party!).

When composing your poem, don't worry too much about rhyming your words. Our writer friend Jonathan informs us that, when it comes to poetry,

"It's rhythms, not rhymes,
that are important
most of the times."

BUNNIES IN THE GARDEN

(from page 50)
Quilt Size: 60" x 80"

This is by far our most involved quilt. It's not super difficult, but you should be forewarned that there's a lot of detail in this quilt. On top of the regular piecing and quilting, there's a sun, a moon, five clouds, 10 radishes, 10 turnips, 10 carrots (including one big one with a zipper), 10 spring onions, 40 flowers, 45 holes (including one that's a tunnel for that big carrot) and, of course, two fish.

But, for kids (and adults like us), this quilt is a dream. There's counting and playing and learning about zippers and buttons and holes and learning about night and day and learning about growing and life and…

Materials & Cutting

We used a lot of scraps!

Material	Approximate Amount	Use
Assorted Blue Scraps	60" x 40"	the sky
Assorted White Scraps	30" x 30"	the clouds and top half of the border
Assorted Scraps	60" x 10"	the hills
Assorted Green Scraps	40" x 40"	the flower garden background
Assorted Scraps	40" x 20"	the flowers
Assorted Brown Scraps	4 pant legs' worth	the vegetable garden
Assorted Polar Fleece™	50" x 40"	the vegetables and bunnies
Unbleached Cotton	3 of 4½" x 50"	the lower half of the border
	60½" x 80½"	the backing
7-oz Batting	2 of 60½" x 80½"	one for the quilt and one for the clouds, flowers, hills, garden rows, etc.
Large White Buttons	8	the clouds, sun and moon
Assorted "Orphan" Buttons	80	the flower centers
10" orange zipper	1	the big carrot

TOTAL Unbleached Cotton = 4 yd (45" width) / 3.5 m (110 cm width)

As usual, all materials were washed, tested for colorfastness and pressed. For the sky, we used cotton, cotton/polyester blends, linen, fun fur, terry cloth, nylon and even a bit of silk. For the hills, we used corduroy and ribbed materials to create the effect of rows in planted fields.

In the foreground are the four rows of the vegetable garden. For these, we used four different brown pant legs. Perspective in the landscape is achieved by shapes becoming smaller toward the horizon. For the flower garden background, we chose just three cottons in subdued colors so that they wouldn't detract from the flowers. The flowers themselves came from vibrantly colored scraps. These scraps can be small, anywhere from 2½" to 5" circles.

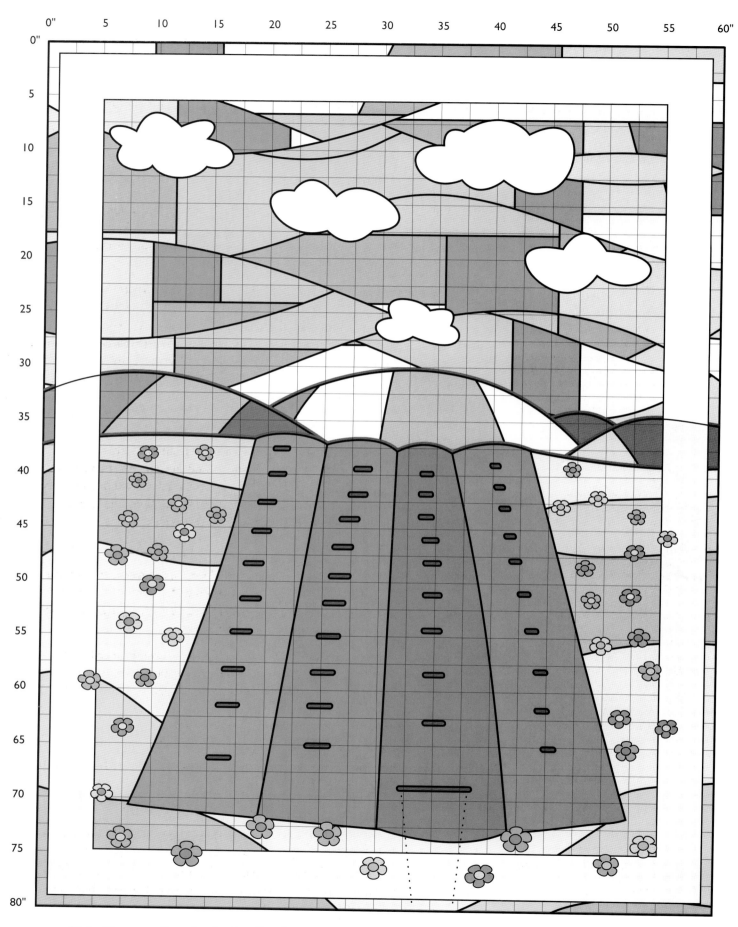

Main Diagram - **Bunnies in the Garden**

Piece the sky with what scraps you have.

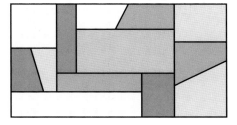

Cut a wavy line.

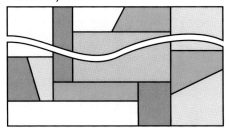

Rotate cut piece 180°. Use it to mark and cut a second line. Now you have 3 pieces.

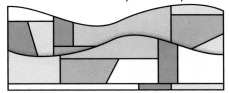

Rearrange the pieces.

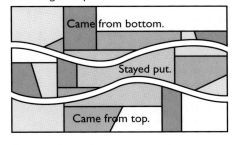

Came from bottom.

Stayed put.

Came from top.

Piece back together using curved seam piecing.

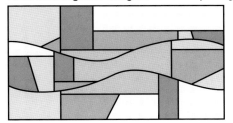

Repeat a few more times.

(Figure 1)

Note: You need to make all of the vegetables before you make the holes for them. See step 12.

For the vegetables and bunnies, we chose Polar Fleece™ because it is stretchy, it turns right side out through small holes easily and it allowed us to leave unfinished edges. Of course it also makes for cute vegetables and cuddly bunnies.

You'll notice that the Materials & Cutting table lists only approximate amounts of material. Very little of this quilt was made to precise geometric dimensions, so watch for cutting information throughout the piecing instructions.

Piecing

1

Piecing the Sky   The finished size of the sky is 50" wide by 25" deep. It was pieced with a technique that is unique to this quilt (see Figure 1). Start by randomly piecing together scraps of salvaged blue fabric until you have a piece that is 55" wide by 35" deep.

Next, cut a wavy line across the top half of the sky. Turn the top piece 180° and use it as a guide to cut the same wavy line out of the bottom half of the sky. Now piece the sky back together, but with the top piece at the bottom and the bottom piece at the top (see page 59 for ideas on "Curved Seam Piecing"). Repeat this step three or four times and you will have created a sky that has nice lines to it and looks as though it was a real challenge to piece. The sky should end up slightly oversized, which is fine, as we will take advantage of this later.

2

Piecing the Hills   When piecing the hills we tried to create the effect of a patchwork of far-off fields with lines converging toward the horizon, as shown in the quilt layout. Piece each hill separately first. Attach the hills to the bottom of the sky using curved seam piecing. Start with the furthest hill and proceed to the closest hill. The hills should extend as wide as the oversized sky.

3

Sew a faced hole in the sky in the horizon where the sun (and moon) will set (see Figure 2). You'll be sewing a lot of these, so consult the "Techniques" section on "Inset Frames" (page 61). The holes in **Bunnies in the Garden** are unique in that they don't have a bottom piece. Rather, they are pockets.

Use a large piece of material for the facing and sew a slot-shaped hole. When the facing is pushed through the slot hole, it naturally forms a flat pocket. Stitch the facing closed. For the sun/moon, make the hole 4½" wide and the pocket 4½" deep.

4

Piecing the Vegetable Garden   Piecing the vegetable garden is a breeze. Piece together four pant legs, which are roughly 36" long and 12" wide in the foreground and 6" wide in the background.

5

Lay out the vegetables onto the garden in rows, with the smallest vegetables in the background and the biggest ones in the foreground. Mark where you wish to put the 40 holes. Then, for each vegetable, make a slot pocket that is specifically shaped for that vegetable. They don't have to be exact, but you want the vegetables to be snug so that they won't fall out of their holes.

The hole for the giant carrot is special. This hole will end up opening to the edge of the quilt, i.e., the tip of the carrot will stick out of the bottom of the quilt. Our suggestion is that you leave this hole until the end of the piecing (Step 11).

6

Piecing the Flower Garden The size of the flower garden should be made to fill from the edge of the vegetable garden to about 2" beyond where the border starts. At first we pieced the garden with straight horizontal lines. It looked too rigid, so we switched to gently curved horizontal lines. Again, we don't suggest a precise pattern. Simply randomly piece your green fabrics together and you will create a nice natural effect.

7

We wanted to have a few secret spots for our bunnies to hide in the flower garden, so we sewed four or five slot holes just the right size for them.

8

Stitch the flower garden to the vegetable garden. Attach the vegetable and flower gardens onto the base of the hills. Using curved seam piecing, we shaped bumps at the end of each garden row to give them some perspective.

9

Piecing Two Borders For the border, we used cream around the garden and hills (for a warm effect) and white around the sky (for a cooler effect). The finished width of the border is 4", so the pieces should be cut to a 4½" width. For our quilt, the finished inside dimensions of our border were 50" x 65". Because of all the curved seam piecing, you may need to adjust these dimensions to fit your quilt.

10

Lay out the quilt top and mark a straight line ¼" outside of where you want the border to go. Piece together the two side panels of the border. Lay the border on the front of the quilt, right sides together. Line the border up with the marked line so that the transition from cream to white matches the hill-sky transition. Stitch the side borders in place. Trim 1" to 2" from the pieced front and save this for the outermost border. Repeat the process for the top white panel and the bottom cream panel of the border.

From the trimmings of the step above, you will make the outer border. Using the trimmings in this way allows the outer border to reflect what is happening inside the wide border. You will need to add to the trimmings to make them long enough. Sew the narrow colored border onto the wide border. Alternately, you could reserve the narrow colored border to bind the quilt in a traditional manner.

11

With the two borders in place, you can now go back and put in the hole for the big carrot. Don't close this hole off. Rather, taper it toward the edge of the quilt, as shown in the Main Diagram.

Choose a location for your sun/moon pocket.

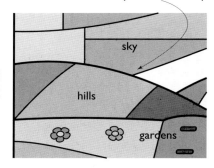

Choose fabric for the slot hole.

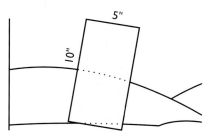

5"

10"

Stitch in the slot.

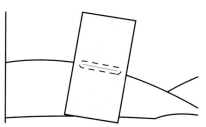

Use a seam ripper to cut the slot inside the stitching.

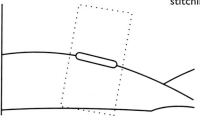

Push piece through hole and flip over to back.

Press flaps together and sew them making a pocket. Keep pieced front out of the way.

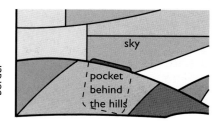

(Figure 2)

Piecing the Bunnies, Flowers, Clouds, Vegetables, Etc. Almost every one of the 100 attachments to this quilt is unique. It's not possible for us to describe them all here. We'll briefly describe how to make them, then let you fend for yourself! Good luck.

Flowers are inverse batt stitched in circles and then turned through a slit in the back. An "orphan" button (a button with no brothers or sisters) is stitched to both sides using embroidery cotton. Before the embroidery cotton is tied off, it is used to form petals by gathering in the edge of the circle.

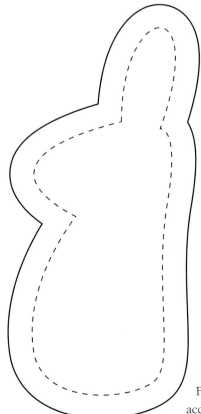

This is a template for both the sun and the moon. For the sun, stitch a buttonhole in the back that is the same size as the buttonholes for the clouds. With right sides together, stitch the front and back of the sun together. Turn right side out through the buttonhole in the back. The moon is made in the same way.

Clouds are inverse batt stitched and then turned right side out through a horizontal slit in the back (see "Inverse Batt Stitching," page 60). A buttonhole is then stitched through the cloud, covering the slit.

Cut out the two sides of each bunny from Polar Fleece™ scraps. Stitch accenting fabric on outside edges of both ears, clip corners and flip through to outside. With right sides together stitch around the bunny body (body only). Turn the bunny right side out through the hole at the top of his head. Loosely stuff the bunny. Hand-stitch the base of the ears together. Use an accenting color for a tail. We made 11 bunnies.

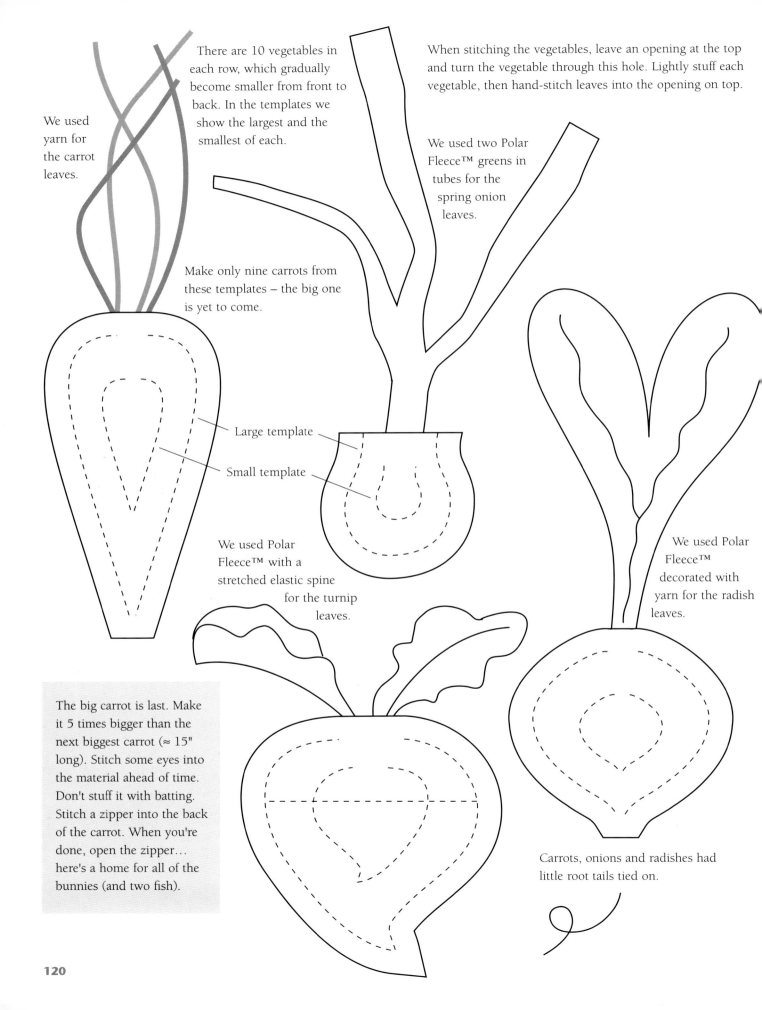

There are 10 vegetables in each row, which gradually become smaller from front to back. In the templates we show the largest and the smallest of each.

When stitching the vegetables, leave an opening at the top and turn the vegetable through this hole. Lightly stuff each vegetable, then hand-stitch leaves into the opening on top.

We used yarn for the carrot leaves.

We used two Polar Fleece™ greens in tubes for the spring onion leaves.

Make only nine carrots from these templates – the big one is yet to come.

Large template

Small template

We used Polar Fleece™ with a stretched elastic spine for the turnip leaves.

We used Polar Fleece™ decorated with yarn for the radish leaves.

The big carrot is last. Make it 5 times bigger than the next biggest carrot (≈ 15" long). Stitch some eyes into the material ahead of time. Don't stuff it with batting. Stitch a zipper into the back of the carrot. When you're done, open the zipper… here's a home for all of the bunnies (and two fish).

Carrots, onions and radishes had little root tails tied on.

Quilting

13

The garden rows should stand out a bit, so cut a piece of batting in the shape of your vegetable garden. Set this piece in place on top of the garden. You should be able to feel where the slot holes for the vegetables are. Mark these locations. Take the batting and cut slits in it for the vegetable holes. Set the batting in place under the garden and push the holes through the slits in the batting. Now the vegetables will all stand up!

14

Pin a full piece of batting behind the pieced front. As usual, it's a good idea to work with an oversized piece of batting that can be trimmed after quilting. Quilt along the seams of the garden rows and the lines of the hills. Quilt some wavy horizontal lines into the sky, much like the lines you used to cut and piece the sky. The remainder of the quilting is done after the backing is put on.

When quilting, make sure not to quilt any of your holes shut.

Finishing

15

We stitched a counting poem into the backing of the quilt before we cut the backing to size. Pin the backing to the pieced front, right sides together. Stitch around the edge of the quilt, leaving an opening where the big carrot hole sticks out. Turn right side out through this hole and press flat. Finish the edges of the carrot hole by hand or by topstitching on the front and back, but don't close the hole! Quilt along the seam on the inside of the border. Again, don't stitch the holes shut (e.g., the big carrot hole).

16

Scatter the flowers around the flower garden. Place the smallest ones close to the hills and the biggest ones in the foreground. Let a few of them drift onto the border. Tie them onto the quilt with embroidery cotton. Use a single loop through one side of the flower and through all layers of the quilt.

Tying the flowers onto the quilt leaves them free to flip over, and change colors!

17

Sew some buttons into the sky for the clouds, sun and moon. Stitch them with embroidery cotton through all layers of the quilt.

Your Quilt

Believe it or not, this is our second **Bunnies in the Garden** quilt. Although we started out with the same idea in mind, this quilt ended up quite different from the other. The first one was simpler than this one, yet just as beautiful. Your quilt will be yet another beautiful variation on the theme. We hope that if you do make a quilt like this one, you'll send us a photo of the finished product!

LAST WORDS

Quilts can require a lot of work. There's designing, preparing fabric, cutting, piecing, appliquéing, and then there's the quilting. Even after the quilting is complete, there's still binding or finishing work to be done. Now, if you put all of these steps together in order to create a functional work of art – for, say, a queen-size bed – well then, it can require a lot of work. It would be wonderful if all this work would happen without any problems, without any mistakes. However, despite best intentions, little tragedies do occur.

QUILT WOES

Setbacks are to be occasionally expected in the quilting process; we're only human, after all. However, we believe that the final quilt is shaped by our dreams, our work and our mistakes. Our mistakes certainly make us more humble. And overcoming our mistakes or setbacks often makes the final quilt all the more meaningful.

So, what do we mean by **quilt woes**?

Because we develop our own designs, we do a lot of exploratory work, or "soul stitching." This is a continual learning experience, and there are a lot of revisions, alterations and even a few abandonments in the process. (We never throw out any scraps of material, but we certainly throw out ideas.) This sort of trial and error is not what we mean by quilt woes.

Neither do we consider a quilt woe to be an oversight, such as not noticing that the bobbin ran out of thread a while ago during a beautifully executed, tricky bit of sewing. For us, a quilt woe is something a little bigger. A quilt woe is something untoward that might have been prevented with a little carefully placed foresight. Here, then, are two examples of our quilt woes, given in order of increasing tragedy. Commiserations are welcome.

Baby Bear Hug versus the Washing Machine

Baby Bear Hug is one of those projects in which we completed the quilting before the backing went on. In this case, it was because the backing was a very rich-looking faux fur. We got the most realistic-looking faux fur in town, and it wasn't cheap. So, we were a little protective of that particular piece of material. We took a small piece of the fur to test in the washing machine before subjecting it to suds and water in its entirety. The results were zero shrinkage and the dye remained colorfast. It was hard to tell, but we thought that maybe, possibly, the test piece had lost just a hint of its exquisite luster. Actually, we thought it probably hadn't lost any of its luster and that we were just being critical or paranoid. However, because the test showed that there was no shrinkage, we decided not to prewash the fun fur in order to leave it fresh and new for photography.

Back to the quilting. We pieced the front of the quilt and then marked the quilting lines using a pencil. We use an 8B or 9B pencil so that it will wash out easily. The quilting was finished through the batting, and the rich fun fur backing was about to go on, when we hesitated. We thought it would be clever to wash the front of the quilt before sewing on the backing. We forgot about the exposed batting.

We already knew that washing machines and exposed batting don't mix. I mean, the washing machine came out fine. On the other hand, the quilted front came out in a little ball. The batting was all knotted up in loose threads from the raw edges of the material. It was a major heartbreak.

Slowly and delicately, we disentangled that quilted front and extricated the batting from the knotted thrums. A little ironing here and a little stitching there, and the baby bear was all better.

Moral of the story: Don't count your bear cubs before they're washed.

Life Is Sweeping Through the Spaces versus Carmen

We like all of our quilts, but **Life Is Sweeping Through the Spaces** might well be our favorite one. It's odd, then, that two of our biggest woes happened with this quilt. We completed **Life Is Sweeping Through the Spaces** early on, and we decided to show it to some friends, including Barb, who was babysitting Carmen.

Now Carmen was a cute little thing: a caramel-colored poodle pup. The reason that Carmen was being babysat is a story all in itself, but it's sufficient to say that Carmen's family was dealing with their own tragedy, and Carmen was displaced and seeking a little attention.

As we were showing the quilt to our friends, Carmen sat unnoticed on the sidelines. The quilt was laid out on the floor, and everyone was admiring it and asking questions. Suddenly Barb let out a gasp. We turned, only to find Carmen squatting in the middle of the quilt. John dove and caught most of Carmen's pee, but not all of it. Barb was horrified and swept Carmen away. We quickly mopped up the rest of the poodle puddle. The whole thing would have been hilarious if it hadn't been so awful.

It would be nice if this were the end of the story, but it's not. After sponging the quilt top clean, we brought in some of the finest noses we knew. No one could detect any odor. Okay, we thought, just give the quilt a quick wash to ensure there's no trace of Carmen left, and it will be as good as new. We took the quilt to an oversized machine in a laundromat and washed it. It was only after the wash that we noticed that one of the materials had bled green into the white clouds.

We have since contained the problem using Synthrapol™ (see "Basic Steps in Quilt-Making," page 57). It took us a lot of time and a lot of agonizing. Still, we think the quilt turned out beautifully.

Moral of the story: Hell hath no fury like a poodle scorned.

ACKNOWLEDGMENTS

Well, did you really think we did it all by ourselves? Everyone in our lives (and a few off the street) helped in some way – donating fabric, helping with ideas, lending us their expertise, listening to endless deadline stories and in general lending us a ton of support. We wish to thank everyone.

fabric   To Robin, Gillian, Devon, Betty, Adela, Jo, Megan Fay, Kerri, Joy, Susan, Ellen, and Allison – thank you for the bags of old clothes and scraps of fabric. We got so much material it was impossible to keep track of where it all came from.

buttons   To the owner of Button Button – thank you for the orphan buttons and especially for Camembert's new green eye (see page 35). Also to Juliet – thank you for releasing Robear (page 4) to be together with Camembert again after 9 long years of being held hostage.

button holes   To Meredydd – thank you for the loan of your machine to do the button holes in Budding Poet. Without it we would have been swamped, so we owe you.

editing   To Gail and Rachelle – thank you so much for your editing. We think the book reads much more good now. Extra thanks to Rachelle for considering us for this project in the first place (and for removing Jan's favorite line from the book "Colorfast – my ass!").

poetry   To Ryan, Naoko, Jonathan and Emily Carr – thank you for adding poetry to the quilts. As well, we should thank Ted, Devin, Lenore and Dale – you were the inspiration for some of the poems. All poems in the book not specifically credited were written by us (John Streicker & Jan Thompson).

fortunes   To everyone at the Glass Onion art studio and their friends – thank you for the fortunes in Fortunate and the words in Budding Poet. You're all invited to dinner to pull a fortune.

photographs   To Jonathan, David, Jo, Susan, Dale, Jamie, Ellen, Jüliska and Scott – thank you for all your help on the photography in the book. It was a lot of work and the results are amazing. Also to Cole – thanks for the loan of the cool cars and stuff for the Playland photo.

camera   To Underhill Geomatics Ltd. – thank you very much for the loan of your Pentax 645 camera. It was invaluable for photographing the quilts.

everything   To everyone listed above, all of the Thompsons, all of the Streickers and many others – you provided ideas and encouragement. Quilting, writing, rewriting, photographing, drawing, designing – in general creating this book has taken so much effort. Your contributions and faith made it possible. Thank you everyone.

kitchen sink   To Jonathan and David – you supplied ideas, poetry, words, criticism, editing, advice, office space, vision, cookies, not to mention all of the photography, all of the book design and even a pair of shorts to cut up for material. Wow! They did all of this for little more than our thanks. And so, thank you David, thank you Jonathan. We hope you realize how much we appreciate your help.

love   To Kerri, Sean and Dale – thank you for your extra inspiration and love – xo Jan.
To Susan – you make life wonderful – xo John.

INDEX